IN AMERICAN HISTORY

JAMESTOWN, JOHN SMITH, AND POCAHONTAS IN AMERICAN HISTORY

Judith Edwards

Enslow Publishers, Inc.

40 Industrial Road   PO Box 38
Box 398   Aldershot
Berkeley Heights, NJ 07922   Hants GU12 6BP
USA   UK

http://www.enslow.com

Library of Congress Cataloging-in-Publication Data

Edwards, Judith, 1940–
   Jamestown, John Smith, and Pocahontas in American history / Judith Edwards.
      p. cm. — (In American history)
   Includes bibliographical references and index.
   Summary: Traces the dangers and adventures surrounding the history of the first permanent British settlement in America, highlighting the roles played by John Smith, Pocahontas, and other individuals.
   ISBN 0-7660-1842-3
   1. Jamestown (Va.)—History—Juvenile literature. 2. Jamestown (Va.)—Biography—Juvenile literature. 3. Smith, John, 1580–1631—Juvenile literature. 4. Pocahontas, d. 1617—Juvenile literature. 5. Virginia—History—Colonial period, ca. 1600–1775—Juvenile literature.
   [1. Jamestown (Va.)—History. 2. Smith, John, 1580–1631. 3. Pocahontas, d. 1617. 4. Virginia—History—Colonial period, ca. 1600–1775.] I. Title. II. Series.
      F234.J3 E38 2002
      975.5'4251—dc21
                                                                              2001003002

Printed in the United States of America

10 9 8 7 6 5 4 3 2 1

To Our Readers: We have done our best to make sure all Internet addresses in this book were active and appropriate when we went to press. However, the author and the publisher have no control over and assume no liability for the material available on those Internet sites or on other Web sites they may link to. Any comments or suggestions can be sent by e-mail to comments@enslow.com or to the address on the back cover.

Illustration Credits: Courtesy Maurice du Pont Lee, reproduced from *Dictionary of American Portraits,* published by Dover Publications, Inc., in 1967, p. 110; Courtesy Virginia State Library, reproduced from *Dictionary of American Portraits,* published by Dover Publications, Inc., in 1967, p. 74; Engraved by Charles Pye after a painting by Sir Antonio More, reproduced from *Dictionary of American Portraits,* published by Dover Publications, Inc., in 1967, p. 20; Enslow Publishers, Inc., pp. 10, 84, 106; Jamestown-Yorktown Foundation, pp. 6, 28, 33, 40, 52; Judith Edwards, pp. 11, 48, 57, 67, 75, 99, 102, 115, 116, 117, 118; Reproduced from *Dictionary of American Portraits,* published by Dover Publications, Inc., in 1967, pp. 32, 87.

Cover Illustration: Judith Edwards; Reproduced from *Dictionary of American Portraits,* published by Dover Publications, Inc., in 1967.

★ CONTENTS ★

1   Three Ships Come Sailing In   5

2   New Worlds to Conquer   14

3   Crossing the Ocean Blue   24

4   Captain Smith and Powhatan   30

5   Pocahontas Helps   39

6   Captain Smith in Charge   51

7   The Starving Time   69

8   John Rolfe and Tobacco   81

9   A New Werowance Makes Plans   ..   92

10   Jamestown Settles Down   98

11   Jamestown Moves On   105

12   Jamestown Revisited   114

    Timeline   119

    Chapter Notes   121

    Further Reading and Internet
      Addresses   126

    Index   127

THREE SHIPS COME SAILING IN

Jamestown, in the Tidewater region of Virginia, has the same serene beauty today that it held back in 1607. Approached from the James River—a wide, calm expanse of water flowing between low-lying shores—Jamestown appears peaceful and secure. Because the water is deep near the shore, boats can anchor close and safe. The vegetation is lush—though now there are manicured lawns edging the swampy forests. As in 1607, when three ocean sailing ships made their way up the river, Jamestown, seen from the river, appears deserted. A few towers now rise above the horizon that was unbroken in 1607, but the sense of peace is unmistakable.

This sense of peace, for those aboard the three ships approaching in 1607, would turn out to be an illusion. In choosing to settle at Jamestown, they had made a terrible choice.

Arrival

On a beautiful, balmy spring day in May 1607, three ships sailed into a small harbor on a river that the area's

The Susan Constant *(replica pictured) was one of the three ships that brought the first English settlers to Jamestown.*

native inhabitants called the Powhatan. The men looking shoreward from these ships were subjects of King James I of England. They had arrived to make this land their own. They named the river the James, after their king. On May 13, 1607, the flagship *Susan Constant*, the smaller *Godspeed*, and the smallest ship, the pinnace *Discovery*, lay in the deep water close to shore.

The shore was almost an island, about two miles long and one mile wide. Only a thin ribbon of land connected the peninsula at its western end to the mainland.

To the 104 settlers and the 40 seamen who would eventually return to England, the area had several good qualities. Because it was almost completely surrounded by water, it seemed as if it would be easy to defend against American-Indian attacks. The water was deep close to shore, so the men could tie the ships to trees and unload from them without having to use smaller boats to carry the supplies. Perhaps best of all, the Spanish, who were threatened by English efforts to explore and settle in the New World, would be thwarted. Jamestown was fifty miles inland from the Atlantic Ocean. Lookouts could be posted to warn the British settlers well ahead of time about a possible attack from Spanish ships.

Dangers of the Expedition

The obvious safety and convenience, however, may have prevented these adventurous Englishmen from truly looking at this site with an eye to the future.

Instructed by the expedition's backers to settle in "the strongest, most wholesome and fertile place," they could not have chosen a worse site for their settlement.[1] The peninsula's marshes bred multitudes of mosquitoes carrying malaria and other possibly deadly diseases. Those living in the seventeenth century, however, had no knowledge of how diseases were spread. They only found mosquitoes annoying.

The lack of fresh drinking water was another, and probably the worst, health hazard the new colonists faced. Because of the low-lying land, the peninsula had no fresh water springs. The James River itself was brackish—partly salt water. Without fresh water, the settlers would be very susceptible to typhoid and dysentery. In the seventeenth century, there were no antibiotics to cure those diseases.

A third hazard was that the land was the territory of the Paspahegh Indians, who were definitely not subjects of King James I. There was every chance that these people would see the newcomers as a threat. They owed their allegiance to the chief, called the *werowance*, of the Powhatan Indians.

The largest stumbling block to the success of the new English settlement, however, would turn out to have nothing to do with mosquitoes, bad water, or American Indians. It had to do with the men themselves. The majority were gentlemen, who were not used to doing hard work with their hands. Many of these men were the younger brothers and sons of wealthy families, who had not inherited the bulk of the family fortune because they were not the first born. Some of the settlers were trained in crafts, and some were soldiers, better with a gun than a shovel. Most notably lacking were farmers—men who knew how to grow and sustain the food that would keep the settlers alive through the winter.

In the pleasant climate of mid-May in Virginia, however, this problem was far from the minds of the weary travelers. Life aboard ship had been confining. Food often rotted and became full of squirming maggots. Passengers and seamen fell ill and their unwashed bodies stank, and storms left them seasick and longing for dry land. Now they were in a beautiful place. Surely they would be able to trade with the Indians for the food they needed. There would be time to worry about crops and harvests later.

Goals of the Expedition

In the meantime, the new settlers had to begin the work that would prepare for a permanent settlement, with additional colonists arriving in the future.[2] They also had to accomplish three things for the Virginia Company, whose backers had paid for this expedition. King James had granted a charter to the company with several conditions: The settlers were to hunt for the gold that was supposedly abundant in the New World; they were to search for the colonists of nearby Roanoke, who had disappeared with hardly a trace several years earlier; and they were to seek out a Northwest Passage to China. Rumors said that the

China Sea was just a few days' walk to the west. The Englishmen had no idea that North America spans thousands of miles and ends at the Pacific Ocean.

Leaders Are Chosen

When the three ships set out from Blackwall, London, in late December 1606, the captain carried sealed orders from the Virginia Company. These orders, which were to be opened only after a site for settlement was chosen, would tell the settlers who was to be on the resident council, which would govern the colony.

The soon-to-be leaders had quarreled among themselves on the trip from England. They were an odd assortment of individuals, peoplewhose differing social positions at home in England were bound to lead to misunderstandings. There was a distinct class system in England in the seventeenth century.

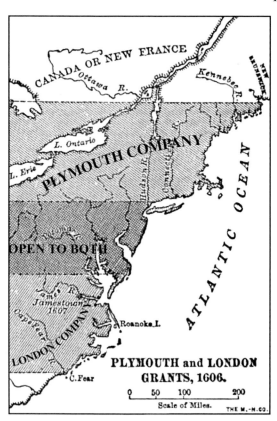

PLYMOUTH and LONDON GRANTS, 1606.

The London and Plymouth Companies made up the Virginia Company. The Virginia Company sponsored the Jamestown Settlement.

John Smith would prove to be Jamestown's most outstanding leader.

Captain John Smith was the son of a farmer from Lincolnshire and had gained a reputation as a brave and hardy soldier. Edward Maria Wingfield, also a well-respected soldier, was a wealthy gentleman of higher social rank, who did not like John Smith.[3] During the voyage Wingfield was offended at what he felt was Captain Smith's lack of respect for his betters. A trumped-up charge of mutiny landed Smith in confinement throughout the voyage. What the other leaders—George Kendall, known to be keeping tabs on the leaders for King James, Captain Christopher Newport, Captain Bartholomew Gosnold, and two other mariners, John Martin and John Ratcliffe—thought about this treatment of Smith is not recorded.[4]

When the sealed orders were opened, to Wingfield's dismay, Captain Smith had been appointed to the council.

SOURCE DOCUMENT

NOW FELL EVERY MAN TO WORK, THE COUNCIL CONTRIVE THE FORT, THE REST CUT DOWN TREES TO MAKE PLACE TO PITCH THEIR TENTS; SOME PROVIDE CLAPBOARD TO RELADE THE SHIPS. SOME MAKE GARDENS, SOME NETS, ETC. THE SAVAGES OFTEN VISITED US KINDLY. THE PRESIDENTS [WINGFIELD'S] OVERWEENING JEALOUSY WOULD ADMIT NO EXERCISE AT ARMS, OR FORTIFICATION BUT THE BOUGHS OF TREES CAST TOGETHER IN THE FORM OF A HALF MOON BY THE EXTRAORDINARY PAINS AND DILIGENCE OF CAPTAIN KENDALL.[5]

John Smith described the early days of the founding of Jamestown.

Elected president of the council, Wingfield was able to veto Smith's seat on the council, but not to put him in jail or punish him. This petty rivalry would lead to a great deal of trouble and tragedy.

Captain Christopher Newport was chosen to lead a small expedition up the James River, while most of the men stayed behind to clear land and build a fort. Newport included Captain Smith in the group of twenty-one men who would go with him.

Beginning the Work of Settlement

At the site of the new settlement, trees were being cut down, land cleared for tents, and gardens dug. Nets were made to catch fish. Timber and sassafras trees were cut to load onto the ships that would return to England. At first, Wingfield dragged his heels about building a fort, saying it would break a company order that the settlers should "not offend the naturals [American Indians]."[6] However, a sudden Paspahegh attack made the need for protection obvious, and the triangular fort, fitted with artillery, was finished by mid-June.

That skirmish was a hint of things to come. The history of the early years of Jamestown is a tale of two empires—American-Indian and English—fighting for dominance over the James River and the land around it.[7] Although Jamestown became the first permanent English settlement in what would later become the United States, it also began the decline of the Algonquian-speaking peoples, including the Powhatan Indians.

NEW WORLDS TO CONQUER

Over five hundred years before Christopher Columbus sailed west, Europeans had enjoyed and desired the exotic jewels, silk, and spices of Cathay, the name they used for China. By A.D. 1100, there were many caravan routes to China and to such countries as Egypt, the Spice Islands, Ceylon, India, and Persia. These mostly overland routes were dangerous. Roads were bad and robbers were numerous. Columbus's voyage was spurred by the great desire to find a less dangerous sea route to reach the Asian countries and their fabled goods.

When Christopher Columbus landed at islands in what became known as the Caribbean Sea, the age of discovery in the New World was launched. Columbus had come upon the West Indies, so named because he believed he was nearing India. With his voyage, the treasure hunt was on.

Nations Compete for the New World

Because Columbus had sailed under the Spanish flag, Spain claimed first rights to the New World. Spanish *conquistadors*, a Spanish word for *conquerors*, defeated native peoples and returned to Spain with gold.

Tales of fabulous wealth excited Europeans, and the business of privateering—attacking enemy vessels with privately owned ships—grew. Spanish ships sailing back across the Atlantic from the New World were considered fair game by the English and other privateers. Not only was there the danger of attack by privateers to make other nations think twice about exploring America, but since Spain dominated this new land as far north as what is now Georgia, the English would have to go farther north to seek a water route to Asia.

In 1497, John Cabot and his son, Sebastian, left Bristol, England, on a search for the Northwest Passage to Asia. They discovered the far-northern islands of Newfoundland and Cape Breton. Like Columbus, who was an Italian citizen who had sailed under the flag of Spain, John Cabot, who was originally from Genoa, Italy, sailed under the English flag. Their discovery spurred English fishermen to descend upon this new land. Staying long enough to preserve the fish they caught, some of these Englishmen from the western part of Great Britain decided to settle.[1]

Jacques Cartier, a French navigator, sailed to North America in 1534 and explored the Saint Lawrence River Estuary, located in today's northern Canada. His discovery of these harsh northern lands and the surrounding waters brought whale oil to Europe as a commodity. Recent shipwreck and settlement discoveries have shown that Basque fishermen from France were processing whale oil in the Labrador region of northeastern Canada as early as 1540.[2] English fishermen soon followed.

With all this new shipping activity, trade increased in the sixteenth century. In England, agricultural methods changed and new large commercial landowners drove many small farmers out of business.[3] A country-wide restless dissatisfaction with life in England encouraged the idea of founding colonies in the New World. The main commodity in sixteenth-century England was wool. Shipping raw wool to weavers in the prosperous European country of Flanders was considered the way to wealth in England.[4] A growing wish for new markets for this raw wool was a further reason to explore the New World.

Rival nations of England were quickly laying claim to other lands rich in natural resources. The Portuguese claimed Brazil, all of Africa and India, and lands east to Japan. Spain, by decree from the pope of the Catholic Church, owned land from Chile to Mexico's Rio Grande river, all of the Caribbean, and north on the North American continent as far as present-day Georgia. Naturally, English Protestants felt that the Spanish and Portuguese claims were unfair, unjust, and illegal. War between Roman Catholic Spaniards and Protestant Englishmen broke out in the late sixteenth century and made the seas even more dangerous routes of travel.

Inspired by the 1507 writings of Amerigo Vespucci, who explored the coast of South America,

Englishman Sir Thomas More wrote a political essay called *Utopia*. Printed in 1516, *Utopia* was about a mythical island and its perfect government. More's essay inspired plans to start a British settlement in North America.

More's brother-in-law, John Rastell, commanded a fleet that left London in 1517, bound for the New World. Rastell had no maritime experience, however, and never made it past Ireland. He went back to England and wrote a play about the wonders of inhabiting a new land. His play further kindled the imaginations of the English people. The play is also important for "containing the first-known English usage of the name America."[5] The term America, however, was coined by a German cartographer named Martin Waldseemüller.

The Search for the Northwest Passage

The search for a water route to China was still under way in 1607 when the settlers landed at Jamestown. This search was undertaken by an impressive group of European explorers and navigators. In addition to the Cabots, they included John Rut; Giovanni da Verrazano; Sir Hugh Willoughby, and Richard Chancellor, traveling together; Stephen Borough; Sir Francis Drake; and John Hawkins. Mathematician and astronomer Dr. John Dee believed that northwest and northeast passages through icy northern oceans were possible.

In 1576, a group of English merchants funded a voyage to be undertaken by maritime explorer Martin Frobisher. He set sail with three ships to find the Northwest Passage. One ship sank after reaching Greenland, located in the far north of the Atlantic Ocean, between Europe and North America. Another ship turned back. But Frobisher, on the ship *Gabriel*, sailed west and discovered Baffin Island, in the far northern regions of Canada.

Frobisher was correct in believing that North America was located at the south of a strait he named Frobisher Strait. But like all explorers before him, Frobisher underestimated the size of the American continent. He believed that the northern area of the strait was part of Asia, because the Inuit-speaking peoples living in this far-northern land looked much like natives of Russian Siberia.

Word that gold was in a "blacke stone much like to a sea cole in colour, which by the waight seemed to be some kinde of metall or minerall" guaranteed Frobisher a return trip.[6] The fact that this "gold" turned out to be a myth only made adventurers more determined.

Sir Humphrey Gilbert tried next. He hoped to start a settlement on the far northern island of Newfoundland. This settlement suffered from much the same lack of work capability as would later occur in Jamestown. In addition, the bleakness of the land was not appealing to the settlers. This colonizing attempt lasted only seventeen days before the ships turned toward home. Gilbert himself took two of his ships south to do more exploration. Severe storms overwhelmed the ships. Gilbert's ship went down north of the Azores islands in the Atlantic, about eight hundred miles west of Portugal. He is said to have shouted, "We are as neere to heaven by seas as by land" just before he was seen for the last time.[7]

One of Gilbert's ships, the *Golden Hind*, limped back to Falmouth, England, in September 1583. Sir Walter Raleigh (Note: *Raleigh* can also be spelled *Ralegh*, however, the former spelling will be used for the purposes of this book.), Gilbert's half brother, had been involved in an attempt to colonize the uninhabited coast of Ireland. Gilbert had received a royal patent from Queen Elizabeth I. It contained a "to have and to hold" clause, which meant that any lands he occupied that were not already occupied by other Europeans would be his property.[8] Raleigh petitioned to continue that patent for himself.

Queen Elizabeth encouraged those who wanted to try their hands at expanding English influence in America. Two prominent men of the sixteenth century had great influence on navigators and on Queen Elizabeth's decision to continue this "to have and to hold" patent.

Early Attempts to Colonize

Richard Hakluyt the Elder and Richard Hakluyt the Younger were cousins with the same name. Richard the Elder was a minister who was fascinated by

Sir Walter Raleigh asked Queen Elizabeth I for permission to search for and colonize new lands in America.

the ocean and the possibility of discovering new lands. He believed in the idea of gaining gold and glory for his country. He also hoped to do what he believed was God's work—by converting the native peoples of other lands to Christianity. He read everything he could find on voyages of exploration. In 1582, he published a book called *Divers Voyages Touching the Discovery of America.* This book had enormous influence on the ideas for English expansion. It would be followed by other important books by both Hakluyts. Walter Raleigh turned to him for advice as he made plans for forming an expedition to colonize in North America.

Sir Walter Raleigh would make two colonization attempts in Virginia (named after Elizabeth I, who was called the "Virgin Queen" because she never married). Just after receiving the Gilbert patent, however, he was instrumental in sending two ships under Captains Philip Amadas and Arthur Barlowe to explore land

SOURCE DOCUMENT

THE SOIL IS MOST PLENTIFUL, SWEET, WHOLESOME, AND
FRUITFUL OF ALL OTHER; THERE ARE ABOUT FOURTEEN
SEVERAL SORTS OF SWEET SMELLING TIMBER TREES; THE
MOST PARTS OF THE UNDERWOOD, BAYS AND SUCH LIKE,
SUCH OAKS AS WE, BUT FAR GREATER AND BETTER . . .

THIS DISCOVERY WAS SO WELCOME INTO ENGLAND
THAT IT PLEASED HER MAJESTY TO CALL THIS COUNTRY OF
WINGANDACOA, VIRGINIA.[9]

Captain John Smith describes Virginia in July 1576.

much farther south than Newfoundland. This exploratory trip went through the Canary Islands off the coast of Africa, to Puerto Rico in the Caribbean Sea, north up the coast of Florida to what is now called the North Carolina Outer Banks, through Pamlico Sound, and on to Roanoke Island.

Amadas and Barlowe had wonderful things to say about this new land they called Virginia. They found the natives peaceful and friendly and even brought back two natives with them. Sir Walter Raleigh and Richard Hakluyt helped the captains write a narrative of their journey, and "some authorities have claimed that Walter Raleigh edited Barlowe's account to make it sound more appealing to investors willing to help underwrite his intent to send a second expedition to Virginia and establish a permanent colony there."[10]

A second expedition in September 1585, led by Sir Richard Grenville, began several months after the

Amadas and Barlowe ships returned. This expedition failed in its colonization attempts. Most fascinating was its attempt in 1587 to settle Roanoke Island in Virginia. After many problems, this colony simply disappeared. Historians still debate what happened to Roanoke and its settlers. Roanoke has become famous in history as the Lost Colony. One theory is that the few people who escaped disease, starvation, and Indian attacks actually went to live with local Indians, but were later killed by them in reprisal for later incursions into their land by Jamestown colonists.[11]

Spanish Settlements

From the time that Spanish explorer Juan Ponce de León explored Florida in 1513, both the Spanish and French sent numerous expeditions to explore this land. La Florida, as it was called, included most of what is now the southeastern United States.

These early expeditions were full of bloody battles between rival European countries and between Europeans and American Indians. Only a handful of the combatants lived. One of these survivors, a captive American Indian named Opechancanough, would later be very influential in the story of Jamestown.

Although Jamestown was the first permanent English-speaking settlement in North America, it was not the first European settlement. In 1526, the Spanish first attempted to plant a settlement in what would become the United States.

The first North American settlement, San Miguel de Gualdape, was financed by a Spanish magistrate named Lucas Vásquez de Ayllón. It was located on the South Carolina coast. Indian attacks, disease, and starvation led the few survivors to abandon the colony after its first winter.

This first colony was followed by settlements south of the Carolinas at St. Elena, St. Catherine's Island, and St. Augustine. These were founded in 1565.

News of these early colonists' adventures, and the persistent rumors of beautiful, fertile land and treasures of gold and jewels, circulated throughout Europe in the sixteenth century. Few warnings about the possible pitfalls, other than highly exaggerated horror stories of cannibal natives and hideous sea monsters, reached the ears of ambitious Englishmen. The rush to take advantage of this new way to achieve economic success was on. The promise of a prosperous future was with the risk-takers who sailed away from their homes in England in December 1606.

CROSSING THE OCEAN BLUE

By 1604, when England and Spain ended the war for political dominance that had been going on between them since 1588, England was eager to found colonies in the New World. Even if little gold was found or a Northwest Passage was impossible, English businessmen believed that American colonies made economic sense. Richard Hakluyt the Younger was influential in convincing the men who would become the backers of the Virginia Company to petition King James I, Queen Elizabeth's successor, for a charter to attempt a settlement. Sir Thomas Gates, Edward Maria Wingfield, Sir Thomas Smythe, and Sir John Popham lobbied for a year to obtain a grant of land from the king.

The English Prepare to Colonize America

Forming a business organization that would turn a profit was the sole purpose of the Virginia Company investors. By forming a joint-stock company, those who held the patent could raise the money they needed by selling pieces of the company to those who wanted to support its efforts in the hope of making a profit for themselves. A person with no money could become a servant in order to pay for his share of future profits. This was called indenture. The person agreed to work for another for a certain period of time, in return for payment of the trip to America. Indentured servants were not slaves. They were free after their period of service ended—if they lived that long. This was a risk that many poor Englishmen were willing to take, and it meant that the colony would have a pool of laborers.

SOURCE DOCUMENT

. . . WHEN YOU HAVE DISCOVERED AS FAR UP THE RIVER AS YOU MEAN TO PLANT YOURSELVES, AND LANDED YOUR VICTUALS AND MUNITIONS; TO THE END THAT EVERY MAN MAY KNOW HIS CHARGE, YOU SHALL DO WELL TO DIVIDE YOUR SIX SCORE MEN INTO THREE PARTS; WHEREOF ONE PARTY OF THEM YOU MAY APPOINT TO FORTIFIE AND BUILD, OF WHICH YOUR FIRST WORK MUST BE YOUR STOREHOUSE FOR VICTUALS; THE OTHER YOU MAY IMPLOY IN PREPARING YOUR GROUND AND SOWING YOUR CORN AND ROOTS; THE OTHER TEN OF THESE FORTY YOU MUST LEAVE AS CENTINEL AT THE HAVEN'S MOUTH. THE OTHER FORTY YOU MAY IMPLOY FOR TWO MONTHS IN THE DISCOVERY OF THE RIVER ABOVE YOU . . .[1]

The instructions given for the settlement of Virginia detailed how labor should be organized. Unfortunately, few of the Jamestown settlers would actually be willing to work hard.

The investors took many months to choose possible members for the resident council, those who would lead the colony. They also worked to recruit colonists and choose and outfit ships, filling them with supplies. At a time when only one person in ten could read and when roads were rutted and difficult, how were these colonists recruited?[2] The majority of the first Jamestown colonists came from the city of London, where one quarter of the entire population of England lived, or surrounding counties. Most of Jamestown's younger men came from eastern England river-port towns. These were home bases for the leaders of the settlement effort, so colonists were gathered from among the leaders' family members, neighbors, and friends. Captain Bartholomew Gosnold's home was used for planning meetings for the Virginia Company. He was its chief recruiter.[3]

The Voyage Begins

The three ships—*Susan Constant*, *Godspeed*, and *Discovery*—were set to leave the port of Blackwall, south of London, in November 1606. Unfortunately, the *Susan Constant*, which was the lead, or flagship, of the fleet, crashed into another ship as it was moving into position to head out to the Atlantic. Repairs were made by December 20, and then the ships sailed for the open sea.

Because the ships were dependent on wind conditions, the sailing was delayed once more. They hovered near England for six weeks. When the wind finally picked up, the ships set sail south to the Canary Islands. There, the crew took on fresh water and were able to go ashore for a short time. By March 1607, the fleet had arrived at the island of Martinique, in the Caribbean just north of South America. It stayed there for three weeks.

As the ships headed for the Virginia coast, a violent storm drove them off course. Regaining its bearings, the fleet entered Chesapeake Bay, south of Jamestown, on April 20, 1607. Moving north up the bay, the tired passengers were sure this was the land of Virginia.[4]

Dropping anchor, Captain Christopher Newport and a landing party rowed their longboats (boats that are lowered from the ship to explore shallower water) to shore. They explored the countryside, but ran into attacking American Indians as they were returning to their longboats. There were a few injuries but no fatalities. Still, it was not the welcome the colonists would have liked.

Exploring the Land

Their ships still anchored close to shore, the settlers began explorations along the coast. The ship's carpenters quickly put together a shallop they had brought with them dismantled, for the purpose of sailing in waters close to shore. (A shallop is a small sailboat.)

One of the first discoveries the colonists made was that their ships were actually at the mouth of a large river. They named the land on either side of this river Cape Henry and Cape Charles. At Cape Henry,

The Susan Constant, Godspeed, *and* Discovery *first anchored in the mouth of the James River. Here, modern reproductions of the ships are pictured.*

located at today's Virginia Beach, there were freshwater springs. The colonists, however, did not choose to settle there. Jamestown archaeologist William Kelso explained, "Perhaps assuming these springs would be everywhere along the Virginia inland waterways, the expedition advanced upriver according to the instructions."[5]

They called this river the James, in honor of the king who had granted them their charter. Exploring the south shore of the James River first, and then crossing to the north shore, they met American Indians who were more friendly than those who had attacked them in their first encounter. These Kecoughtan people welcomed the explorers and hosted them for several days before the Englishmen's shallop moved farther up the James.

At another village, named Paspahegh after the tribe who lived there, a group of explorers, including Captain Newport, stayed for several days. The situation was looking good. Most of the natives were friendly, and George Percy, who had traveled farther upriver, believed he had found a good settlement site. He called it Archer's Hope. Though there were abundant game, trees, and fresh water, some of the other leaders believed Percy's choice would be difficult to defend, so they moved on.

Jamestown was not one hundred miles up a navigable river, where the settlers had been instructed to go. It was only fifty miles inland. However, it was somewhat hidden by a peninsula, named Hog Island, from possible attack by the rival Spanish.[6] There did not seem to be any Indians actually living on the site, and the settlers could tie their ships to trees and unload easily. The expedition chose to begin the English settlement at Jamestown.

CAPTAIN SMITH AND POWHATAN

Captain Christopher Newport, admiral of the fleet, was an experienced seaman. It would be his job to take the *Susan Constant* back to England six weeks after the fleet's landing in Virginia to bring back more settlers and supplies for the new colony. Along with Newport's instructions, a sealed box contained the Virginia Company's directives, proclaiming the names of those who would serve on the council.

The directives also included orders to continue to explore up the river. The settlers' main objectives were to find gold and that ever-elusive Northwest Passage. Captain Newport and twenty-one men headed the shallop upriver to begin explorations. Captain Bartholomew Gosnold took twenty men inland to look for minerals. The remaining third of the colonists, and the seamen who would later return to England, stayed in Jamestown to build a fort and plant crops, despite the lateness of the season.

Captain John Smith

"The twenty-second day of May, Captain Newport and myself, with others, to the number of twenty two persons, set forward to explore the river some fifty or sixty miles," wrote Captain John Smith in *A History of the Settlement of Virginia*.[1] Although Smith has been accused of exaggerating his exploits in this book, it is the most important record we have of the early days at Jamestown.

Who was this man with the plain name? He had caused controversy among the Jamestown leaders even before they landed. He would continue to do so during his stay in America. In his dealings with the American Indians, he would save the day for Jamestown several times.

Captain John Smith was a colorful character. He was a small, very intelligent man with a large will and an even larger ego. Before shipping out for Virginia, he had won a reputation as a brave and reckless soldier of fortune in France, the Netherlands, Italy, Austria, and Turkey. He had survived two years as a captive slave in Turkey, going from master to master. He finally escaped by killing his last master, donning the dead man's clothes, and fleeing the country. Despite his desperate situation during his captivity in Turkey, he "carefully noted the manners and customs of the people, their diet, clothing, houses, treatment of slaves, feasts, religion and conduct in war."[2] He would continue this practice in Jamestown, observing both American Indians and colonists. He would leave for posterity very specific, well-written accounts of people and events involved in the settlement of Jamestown.

Although he was not a member of the nobility, John Smith had many skills that served the Jamestown settlement well.

Smith never made the mistake of underestimating the intelligence of the natives of the land the English had arrived to conquer. A master at outsmarting his enemies, he knew that the American Indians were equally crafty and cunning. Not recognizing that fact could be deadly. Smith perhaps read a further layer into one of the directives that emerged from the sealed instructions to the Virginia Company directors: "In all your passages you must take great care not to offend the natives, if you can avoid it, and employ a few of your company to trade with them for corn and all other lasting victuals [food supplies] if they have any."[3]

The Powhatan Empire

Newport's trip upriver more than met the provisions of that directive. The Indians welcomed the English invaders with feasts of fruit, fish, and bread. In return, Newport gave them small goods such as pins, beads, and bells.

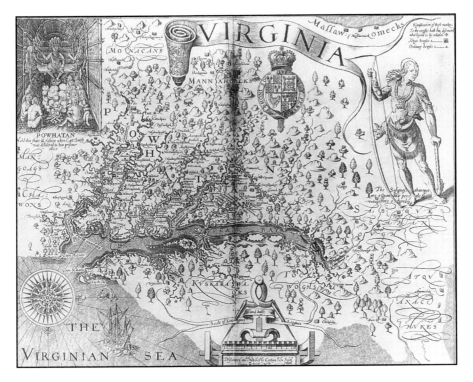

This is a 1612 print of John Smith's map of Virginia, the result of his explorations during his two-and-a-half years in Virginia. It was the first accurate representation of the area.

Proceeding north toward the waterfalls of the James River near present-day Richmond, Newport's group entered the countryside dominated by Powhatan, the big chief, or "werowance," of the far-reaching Powhatan empire. One of Powhatan's sons, Parahunt, whom Newport called Pawatah, was friendly to the travelers. However, one of the Indian guides was puzzled when he heard a great shout from the English that celebrated Newport's placement of a cross on a small island.[4] This ceremony proclaimed James I the king of Virginia. The Indians would not have liked to hear this news. Instead, Newport explained that the cross represented the united forces of Indians and Englishmen, and that the shout was "an expression of the English reverence for Powhatan."[5]

The rest of the English settlers were not to meet this mighty werowance—big chief—until they had lived at Jamestown for six months. The English could not even imagine the true power of Wahunsonacock, who called himself "Powhatan" after the name of his village. Powhatan's empire reached from the Potomac River at the north to the Great Dismal Swamp in the southeast, and west to the falls of the tidal rivers that later gave the Tidewater region of Virginia its name.

Powhatan inherited six area tribes in the last years of the sixteenth century. In about 1597, his combined forces conquered the Kecoughtan people. This tribe, which lived at the mouth of the James River, was large. Its defeat brought great land and wealth into Powhatan's monarchy. A year after the English arrived in Jamestown, Powhatan ruled over some thirty tribes, all of which paid tribute (payments recognizing his dominance) to him as werowance.

In 1607, Powhatan's empire consisted of fourteen thousand subjects, including thirty-two hundred warriors. The werowance installed his relatives as chiefs in different villages. The only tribes in Tidewater free from his domination were the Chesapeake at Cape Henry and the Chickahominy who lived along the river of the same name.

Powhatan ruled with total power over his conquered tribes. His amazing success was the result of a combination of having large numbers of men and his own sharp political understanding.[6] John Smith wrote, "It is strange to see with what great fear and adoration all these people do obey this Powhatan."[7] Smith described Powhatan in detail. His writings were the first, very specific images of the political, social, and religious lives of these American Indians.

Around age sixty when the English arrived in his country, Powhatan was still tall and muscular. His hair was gray and his face looked somewhat sad. He dressed in the same deerskin and moccasins, with a raccoon fur cape, as did his American-Indian subjects. When the English met him, he sat on a throne with his bodyguard of forty warriors around him, as well as many of his one hundred wives. The tribute paid by his tribes he placed in a huge treasure house, guarded by priests and carved demons. He distributed food evenly around his realm, thus ensuring the people's loyalty. If anyone broke his laws, they were punished severely, with torture or death. Historian James Axtell wrote, "Understandably, subjects went out of their way to avoid his displeasure."[8] By the time Jamestown was settled, Powhatan knew about Europeans, and he was not impressed.

During the sixteenth century, ships from France, Spain, and England had regularly entered Chesapeake Bay and traded with Indian tribes. The European crews needed water, firewood, and fresh food. They brought with them diseases such as smallpox and measles to which the Indians had no immunity. These new diseases killed thousands of Indians. As historian James Axtell wrote, "In 1608 Powhatan told the English, with some exaggeration, that he had seen 'the death of all my people thrice, and not one living of those 3 generations, but my selfe.'"[9]

Opechancanough

Powhatan had many wives, children, nephews, and nieces. One of these close relatives, believed to be his younger half brother, was called Opechancanough. This intelligent and fierce warrior, who would inherit Powhatan's empire, figured widely—and disastrously—in the early years of Jamestown.

In 1561, as a young boy, Opechancanough was either captured or allowed by his tribe's leader to sail to Spain with Spanish navigator and soldier Pedro Menendez de Aviles. In Europe, the tall, handsome American Indian was educated in Christianity by priests and taught the Spanish language.[10]

Historian Carl Bridenbaugh believed that Opechancanough not only learned language and the Bible, but also observed the value of diplomacy, patience, and strategic planning.[11] He would bring those skills with him when he returned to America. They would enhance the Powhatan empire and affect the strategies the Indians used to counter the encroaching European invasion. He also saw just how enormous the population of white Europeans was—and how they could affect his own people.

In 1563, Opechancanough, who had been promised a trip back to his home after a few years, accompanied Pedro Menendez de Aviles to Mexico. There, the archbishop (a high official in the Catholic Church) insisted that he remain, fearing Opechancanough would abandon Christianity for his old religion if allowed to return to his homeland. He was placed under the protection of Governor Don Luis de Velasco, who gave Opechancanough his own name—Don Luis de Velasco. King Philip II of Spain finally sent orders that the new Don Luis be allowed to return to his home on the York River in what is now Virginia.

Unfortunately, more delays and storms at sea landed Opechancanough back in Spain once again. Hearing that a party of Catholic missionaries was about to head to America to convert the natives, this politically aware young man suggested to the priests that he go with them to help in the conversion. They agreed.

After spending several months in Havana, Cuba, on September 10, 1570, Opechancanough landed on his home shore, about five miles upriver from what would later become Jamestown.

Within one short month, the name Don Luis was cast aside and Opechancanough re-emerged. It was the custom for the nobility in the Powhatan Indian tribes to take several wives. When the Catholic priests publicly scolded Opechancanough for doing so, the young man renounced Christianity and moved permanently back into his home village. Several months later, he led an Indian attack on the York River mission, near Jamestown, killing the priests. Later reprisals from the Spanish would kill many Indians, but Opechancanough would not be around. He would, however, be back to play a role in John Smith's and Jamestown's history.

While Newport and John Smith were exploring, the remaining third of the Jamestown settlers were digging ground to build a fort and making arrangements to grow and gather food. Barely a month had passed since they landed at Jamestown on May 13, 1607. Perhaps not to "offend the naturals" Edward Maria Wingfield, as director of the colony, did not hurry the men to build the fort.[1] This was to prove a mistake.

POCAHONTAS HELPS

Unfinished Defenses

John Smith, who reported receiving good treatment from the Indians on his upriver trip with Captain Newport, noted that on the return trip, the same Indians who had been friendly earlier now "seemed little to like us."[2] The *Susan Constant* hurried on to the Jamestown settlement. There, the exploring crew found the occupants still reeling from an attack by two hundred to four hundred Paspahegh Indians— depending on whose account one reads—the day before. The settlers, whose building and planting activity showed that they intended to stay longer than for an

A twentieth-century artist painted this depiction of the building of James Fort.

exploratory trip, had accidentally occupied the Paspahegh hunting grounds. The tribe responded with an attack to force the English away.

Because the Jamestown fort was incomplete, it did not yet hold the settlers' artillery. Retreating to the armed *Godspeed*, which was moored close to shore, the desperate and unprepared colonists drove the Paspahegh away by musket and cannonfire.

When the other men returned from exploring, completing and arming the fort became the major consideration. The fort was built in the shape of a triangle with bulwarks—reinforced walls for defense—that could hold artillery.

It was early summer by the time the fort was ready. No further Indian attacks had occurred, and a representative sent from Powhatan promised peace. The settlers were hopeful about the situation.

The Struggle for Power

On July 22, 1607, with boards, sassafras, and a bit of earth that might contain gold loaded on the ships, Captain Newport set sail with the *Susan Constant* and the *Godspeed*. His plan was to reach England as quickly as possible, unload the ships, and bring them right back with additional supplies and colonists. While he was home, he could also give good reports on the colony's progress to the Virginia Company's backers.

However, even before Newport reached England, the well-being of the colony had changed dramatically. The basic problem was leadership. Edward Maria Wingfield, courageous in battle, was no political leader. His continuing hatred of John Smith further divided the members of the council. Wingfield was even accused by other councilors of stockpiling food for himself that should have been shared. He was voted out of the presidency. John Ratcliffe took his place. This, however, did not help matters. Conspiracies were whispered everywhere. Colonist George Kendall, supposedly loyal to King James, was actually accused of causing trouble and shot.

During all of this petty rivalry, the ordinary settlers were left without guidance and long-term planning. Before the end of July 1607, food was already in short supply. Belated attempts to ration grain, even the grain that was full of bugs, was resented. There was simply not enough food to satisfy everyone's hunger. Drinking the semisalty water, which was all that was available, made the men sick. Disease soon set in. The summer turned very hot. George Percy, one of the colony's leaders, described the diseases that took men suddenly. He also said, "but for the most part they died of meere famine. There was never Englishmen left in a forreigne Countrey in such miserie as wee were in this new discovered Virginia."[3] There was no ship to take them to a better spot, and they had no authority to leave the site.

John Smith wrote, "we were plagued with so much famine and sickness, that the living were scarce able to bury the dead."[4] By early September, 46 of the original 104 settlers were dead.

The Paspahegh Indians helped the survivors when they arrived with corn and bread. Fowl heading southward, landing on the river, could be hunted for food. Smith also began a series of short trips to find provisions. On the second of these, council members voted that he should take the *Discovery* upriver to Powhatan to trade for corn. Although Smith's party was harassed along the way by various Indians, he managed to return with ten bushels of corn.

With cooler weather and more food, the men who had survived the famine and disease of summer began to recover their health. The weakened men, these "gentlemen," whose lack of fishing and hunting skills were obvious even before famine and disease became a problem, began to work, under Smith's direction, on finishing houses before the winter. A little of the adventuring spirit returned to the settlers.

Meanwhile, John Smith began to explore more of the area around them. In December, the council sent Smith on a trip to explore the Chickahominy River, about five miles north of Jamestown. Once again he hoped to find the rumored great lake that would lead to China. The results of this trip would become one of the great American legends.

The Adventures of John Smith

One of the difficulties in putting together a clear story of this chapter from the history of the early days of the Jamestown Colony, is that Smith was the only European witness. Never one to be shy about his own role in dangerous situations, this very short, very powerful man of only twenty-seven years, wrote three separate accounts of the events of his trip.

Smith left Jamestown with nine men, to travel up the Chickahominy River. About thirty miles upriver, the barge was blocked by fallen trees. Captain Smith left seven men behind to watch the boat, and set out with two Indian guides from Powhatan's village and a canoe, to hunt and explore further. John Robinson and Thomas Emry also went along.

When they stopped to eat, Smith decided to do some more exploring on his own. He set out with one Indian guide, leaving Robinson, Emry, and one guide to prepare the meal. If other Indians approached, they were told to fire their guns.

Soon, hearing Indian shouts instead of gunshots, Smith tied his Indian guide's arm to his own hand and started back to the camp. Before he could go very far, an Indian arrow nicked his leg. He swung his Indian guide in front of him as a human shield, and faced the Indian attackers. The number of Indians who were shooting at him grew with each version of the story Smith wrote, but presumably neither Smith nor the Indian guide, despite all the arrows fired at them, was seriously hurt.[5] Smith fled with the Indian still attached into Chickahominy Swamp, seemingly with no way out.

Earlier, George Cassen, one of the men who had gone along on Smith's exploring expedition, had wandered away from the barge and was captured by Indians. Under torture, he told the Indians that Smith, Emry, and Robinson were on their way upriver. The Indians found and killed Emry and Robinson. Then they went after Smith. The remaining six men on the barge managed to push out into the river and head for the fort at Jamestown.

December temperatures are normally mild in Virginia. That was not the case in December 1607.

John Smith was not only surrounded by hostile Indians, but he was exposed to the wet and cold, which were quickly becoming intolerable.

The Pamunkey Indians, who surrounded Smith and his still-attached Indian guide, were part of Powhatan's empire. Their tribe numbered over a thousand people. It was their leader, Opechancanough, who captured Smith and assured him that he would not be killed—at least not right away—if he surrendered.[6] This impressive Indian was still tall and strong. After Smith surrendered, he talked at length, through translators, with Opechancanough. They traded information about their people, both American-Indian and English.

Smith bought himself time by giving the powerful chief a compass and explaining its use. Opechancanough took Smith up and down the York River, showing all the local tribes his captured prize. Captain Smith was fed very well, with all the best venison and bread. Smith began to fear that they were fattening him up to eat him.[7]

The first break for Smith came when a man at Opechancanough's hunting camp asked him to cure his son, whom Smith had wounded with a pistol during the American-Indian attack. Smith said that he had special medicines back at the Jamestown fort. If they would let him go fetch them, he would be able to cure the man.[8] The Pamunkey Indians were not about to fall for that. They did, however, let Smith write on a paper, which four of the Indians delivered to the fort. When the Indians returned in three days with the medical supplies, many of them felt Smith had performed magic. Because they had no written language, they had trouble understanding how the marks he had made on the paper had relayed his thoughts to the men at the fort.

Saved by a Legend

Shortly after this incident, Smith was taken to Werowocomoco, Powhatan's chief residence on the York River. Powhatan wanted to know why the English were in Virginia. In turn, Smith wanted to know from Powhatan more about the land. In Smith's first version of these events, Powhatan released Smith after they had this conversation.

According to later versions of Smith's story, there was great feasting when he was delivered to Powhatan. The Indians consulted at length before two large stones were brought into Powhatan's throne room. Smith was then dragged toward the stones. The Indians forced him to lay his head down. They then raised clubs as if they were about to smash them down on Smith's head. It is at this point that Powhatan's favorite daughter, Pocahontas, who was then about ten or twelve years old, ran forward. She put her arms around John Smith's head, and placed her head down on his. The Indians' clubs were put down at Powhatan's command, and Powhatan proclaimed that John Smith should live "to make for him hatchets, and for Pocahontas bells, beads, and ornaments of copper; for they thought him as good at all occupations as they were," according to John

SOURCE DOCUMENT

. . . HAVING FEASTED HIM AFTER THEIR BEST BARBAROUS MANNER THEY COULD, A LONG CONSULTATION WAS HELD, BUT THE CONCLUSION WAS, TWO GREAT STONES WERE BROUGHT BEFORE POWHATAN: THEN AS MANY AS COULD LAID HANDS ON HIM [JOHN SMITH], DRAGGED HIM TO THEM, AND THEREON LAID HIS HEAD, AND BEING READY WITH THEIR CLUBS TO BEAT OUT HIS BRAINS, POCAHONTAS, THE KING'S DEAREST DAUGHTER, WHEN NO ENTREATY COULD PREVAIL, GOT HIS HEAD IN HER ARMS, AND LAID HER OWN UPON HIS TO SAVE HIM FROM DEATH . . . [9]

An excerpt from John Smith's account of his rescue by Pocahontas.

Smith.[10] This statement was clearly a sign of friendship from the chief toward John Smith.

Is this popular legend from America's beginnings just another of John Smith's exaggerations? The scene with Pocahontas did happen, according to scholars such as Ivor Hume, but it was most likely a "carefully staged" show of kindness toward the English by the crafty Powhatan.[11] The very politically aware Indians must have realized that if they killed Smith, one of the English leaders, there would be reprisals from Jamestown. Smith had pointed out to Opechancanough, who had been to Europe, that there were many, many more Englishmen across the ocean.[12]

Pocahontas's actions, staged or spontaneous, sent John Smith back to Jamestown unharmed. Two days

Pocahontas, represented in this statue at Jamestown today, played a vital role in the early years of the English settlement.

after the almost-execution, Powhatan declared friendship for the still-captive John Smith. The Indian chief offered to make Smith chief of a small village, and adopt him as a son, whom he would call Nantaquoid.

Peace With Powhatan—For Now

Smith returned to Jamestown shortly after 1608 began. He was accompanied by Indian guides, who were supposed to return to Powhatan with presents from Smith and his fellow settlers. Included among the presents were to be two cannons called demiculverins. Since these weighed nine thousand pounds, however, Smith noted, "they found them somewhat too heavie."[13] Not only was the weight a problem but Smith almost scared the Indians away completely by firing one of these nonportable gifts. However, the Indians did return to obtain smaller presents from the settlers. Later that week, Pocahontas arrived with an Indian escort, bringing food for the shivering settlers.

Jamestown was once again in a sorry state. Preparations were under way to abandon the colony and board the *Discovery* and sail for England. The leaders, who had fought among themselves while Smith was being dragged from one Indian village to another, were not particularly happy to have him back. Smith actually made the settlers, who considered themselves "gentlemen," work.[14] Gabriel Archer, now a member of the council, joined with President Ratcliffe to condemn Smith for the deaths of Robinson and Emry, the two men who had accompanied him when he had set out with his Indian guide to explore. Smith was supposed to hang the very next day.

It was the return of Captain Christopher Newport from England that saved Smith this time. Sixty new settlers arrived in Jamestown aboard the ship the *John and Francis.* Forty more settlers were aboard a second ship under Newport's command, the *Phoenix*, as well as most of the supplies. That ship lost its way in a fog on Christmas Eve, 1607. Added to the forty survivors from the first three ships that had arrived in Jamestown in May, the new arrivals brought the colony's numbers back up to one hundred. Most of the settlers were in fairly good health.

Captain Newport, realizing the need for Smith's expertise and good relations with the Indians, freed Smith. Newport then took temporary charge as the new settlers left the ships to set up their homes in this new land.

CAPTAIN SMITH IN CHARGE

Captain Newport left his ship to go ashore on a Sunday. He dealt with the continuing political bickering, released John Smith, and got to work making arrangements for the settlers and supplies. On Monday, January 4, 1608, the new arrivals disembarked. Supplies were stored and the fort made ready to house the new arrivals.

On Thursday, January 7, however, a fire broke out in the building where supplies were kept. It soon spread to every house in the fort. By the time the flames were contained, only three houses remained.[1]

The fire was able to spread so rapidly and so disastrously because the houses were built of wattle and daub. Wattle is made of reeds, small branches, and sticks. Daub is clay mixed with sand, straw, and water. The Jamestown houses' roofs were thatched—made of straw. If a fire started in one of these buildings, it burned upward, at very hot temperatures. When the thatch caught fire, it blew outward, igniting other roofs. Sometimes, clay walls could withstand the heat and remain standing, but wooden wall posts often burned to the ground.

This reconstruction of the Jamestown fort shows how life might have been among the early English settlers.

One eyewitness account of the Jamestown fire hinted that the storehouse for munitions and supplies burned first.[2] If this is true, gunpowder would have helped spread the fire in all directions, making it almost impossible to put out.

The terrible fire left both old and new settlers without homes, supplies, or even clothing in the coldest part of winter. The settlers were now in even worse shape than they had been before the supply ships arrived. There was less food, and many more people who had to eat it. Once again, the local Indians saved the unlucky colonists with frequent gifts of food. The American Indians' mixed attitude toward settlers is hard to understand. They seemed to attack the English for a while, then help them at other times. Perhaps the Indians had decided that the Europeans were valuable sometimes—especially when they gave the Indians trade goods such as cooking pots, weapons, mirrors, and guns.

The Jamestown fire also burned the palisade—the wooden fencing—of the fort itself. Both fort and town were not rebuilt until April, after Captain Newport's ships departed once again for England to bring more supplies and more settlers. Left without homes, the settlers either slept on the ships or quickly built rough shelters to get them through the cold months. Many of the already weakened original settlers died from inadequate nutrition that winter.

The Search for Survivors of Roanoke

Captain Newport had arrived with explicit orders from the company directors to try to find any survivors from the "Lost Colony" of Roanoke. Rumors had crossed the sea that people wearing European-style clothing, and living in two-story homes with stone walls, were living south of Roanoke Island. The Virginia Company directors wanted to find out if the rumored survivors were still alive. In February, Newport sent two men with a Paspahegh guide to explore. Unfortunately, the guide abandoned them and took their equipment. They were able to return to Jamestown, but their attempt to find the lost colonists was over.

Later that February, Smith and Newport made a trip to see Powhatan, whose gifts of food were keeping the Jamestown Colony alive. A company of forty Englishmen sailed up the James River and into the York River, wearing full armor, and carrying muskets and swords. It was a peaceful trip, but the English wanted to make sure the Indians knew exactly what would happen if the English soldiers were attacked.

The visitors were treated to much pageantry and feasting in Powhatan's royal village. Powhatan asked to trade not on an item-by-item basis, but in a more respectful, businesslike manner. He wanted the English to display "all our Hatchets and Copper together, for which he would give us corne."[3]

A Run-in With Powhatan

Newport, who had not found the Roanoke survivors, needed to go back to England for more supplies. He departed on April 20, 1608. Before he left, he gave Powhatan twenty swords in exchange for twenty turkeys. After Newport's ship sailed, Powhatan tried to get the same trade deal with Smith, who refused. Smith understood that the price Powhatan wanted for his turkeys was inflated. He was determined to get Powhatan to return trade relations to a reasonable level.

Furious that his supposed friend would deny him, Powhatan ordered the English weapons seized by force. Smith, in turn, chased the Indians and took seven of them captive. The Indians then seized two soldiers who were outside the fort. Instead of buckling under, Smith sent men with muskets and armor out of the fort to fight. The Indians backed down.

Smith told each of his captives that the others had been shot. He even fired a musket to prove it.[4] He told each one that the others had been shot for not telling who was behind all the treachery. Of course, it was Powhatan. Soon, the powerful werowance had decided being nice would be in his best interests, since Smith was toughening up trade agreements. Powhatan sent young Pocahontas to the Jamestown fort, accompanied by her Indian guards, to plead for the Indian prisoners' lives. Smith, as good a politician as Powhatan, released all seven prisoners. He made it known that he was doing so only out of thanks and respect for Pocahontas. Once again, Smith, the most practical leader of the English colony, had assessed a situation realistically and acted. For this skill, he was both respected and envied by the other leaders of the colony.

The *Phoenix* Arrives

Shortly after Newport's April 1608 departure, the *Phoenix*, which had been lost in the fog on Christmas Eve, 1607, appeared in Jamestown harbor. After suffering through severe storms, the ship had been whipped by the wind back to the West Indies. There, the forty survivors rested, repaired the ship, and obtained more food and water.

Most of those aboard the *Phoenix* were healthy, and the supplies they brought were very much needed in Jamestown. Carrying lumber cut by Jamestown settlers, the *Phoenix* set sail for England in July 1608.

At the same time, Smith and fourteen colonists were traveling down the James River, on an open barge. Their mission was to explore Chesapeake Bay. Halfway through the exploratory trip, Smith was wounded in the arm by a stingray, a fish that injects victims with stinging poison through a pointed barb. He had to return to Jamestown to nurse the wound.

There, he discovered that all the recently healthy new arrivals were sick, along with many other settlers. Ratcliffe, still president of the colony, was very much out of favor. Smith actually took over the presidency informally in mid-July.

Because Smith wanted to do more exploring in Chesapeake Bay, however—there was always the hope of finding the legendary Northwest Passage to China—he once again left Jamestown. Smith had his usual hair-raising misadventures and close calls with hostile Indians, but he returned with four hundred baskets of corn. During his absence, he appointed his friend Matthew Scrivener, still recovering from an illness, deputy.

Smith Officially Takes Charge

When Smith returned to Jamestown in September, Ratcliffe was in prison, and the harvest had been successful. However, the supplies held in the storehouses had been ruined by rain, and a great many settlers had died.

As far as modern historians can figure out, the total number of colonists living in Jamestown in September 1608 was about one hundred twenty. These people lived in about twenty houses within the fort.[5] More settlers were expected to arrive with Newport any day, and Smith knew more houses needed to be built. Smith was officially named the Jamestown Colony's president that same month.

Smith was given this honor because he had energetically and with obvious skill organized labor and food supplies to prevent the settlers from starving. However, the new president faced formidable problems.

This wattle-and-daub house was typical of the kind of structure built by the early Jamestown residents.

One of these problems arose because of a decision taken by the council, in regard to Newport's sailors. These men wanted to turn Newport's ship around and go home to England. They did not want to wait around for Newport to hunt for lost Roanoke colonists or to visit Powhatan. To make them happy, the council decided to allow the sailors to "trade privately with the Indians on any terms they liked."[6] The sailors, who still believed the old rumors about the Indians owning large supplies of gold, paid high trade prices for almost anything in order to gain information about where this gold might be. The Indians, who quickly got used to this, came to resent the colonists' trading offers.

As the Indians' disdain grew, food supplies that had once been readily available dwindled. That lack of food, combined with the food consumed by the crew during the nearly four months they stayed at Jamestown, left the colonists hungry. When the ships left, they would take more food with them for the voyage home. When John Smith officially became Jamestown's president on September 8, his first and most important task was to attempt to turn the undisciplined, discouraged colonists into an effective work force.

Smith divided the work force into task groups. One group of men fished, another planted, and another—which included those who considered themselves "gentlemen"—chopped down trees and cut clapboards for building and shipment to England. Everyone was expected to work to repair the fort and build more housing. Smith had a blockhouse built to prevent the theft of trade items. He also trained a large number of soldiers how to fight like the Powhatan people, and taught the Englishmen American-Indian customs and language.

Smith abandoned the rule about not offending the natives. Smith got tough, even ruthless, toward the American Indians. Captains John Martin and George Percy were particularly brutal with Indians, using torture and decapitation to intimidate. Smith himself had a confrontation with Opechancanough, which has been immortalized in an engraving by Robert Vaughan in Smith's *Generall Historie of Virginia*.[7] In the picture, a very small man is gripping a very tall, muscular Indian's scalp lock (the only part of the hair not shaved; coming from on top of the head and worn long, the Powhatan people considered it the bodily representation of the soul). The small man is pointing a gun at the Indian's chest. Smith is promising to kill all the Indians he could find and send their bodies down the river on a barge if Opechancanough did not supply the settlement with corn.

Some corn and other food were gathered from this get-tough stance, however it might have been exaggerated in the picture. The English settlers' new attitude also put a momentary stop to theft and harassment. But these policies left the Indians with resentment and a wish for revenge that would have ill consequences in the future.

To Smith's credit, if the colony hoped to survive at all, someone had to take charge of an out-of-control situation, and do it swiftly and completely. He was very upset when Newport arrived in October with seventy more colonists, including two women, just three weeks after Smith had assumed the presidency. Half of the new settlers were "gentlemen," unused to working with their hands. It seemed that the company directors had learned no lessons from the difficulties caused by their failure to send to Jamestown able-bodied men skilled at hunting and farming.

Newport, who appreciated Smith's skill, never really liked Smith's arrogance. Newport scolded Smith on behalf of the Virginia Company for bringing the colony close to failure. Apparently, the English needed a scapegoat to explain the continued difficulties Jamestown had been facing.

The "Crowning" of Powhatan

Soon after Newport's arrival, he announced that he would be holding a great ceremony to "crown" Powhatan as a royal figure—like a lord or a count who was considered a friend of great royalty in the house of King James I. This idea probably did not fool anyone, least of all Powhatan. When the werowance was asked to come to Jamestown to receive the gifts King James had sent him, Powhatan answered, "If our king has sent me presents, I also am a king, and this is my land; I will stay eight days to receive them. Your father is to come to me, not I to him, nor yet to your fort; neither will I bite at such a bait."[8] Powhatan, whom the Europeans considered a "savage," was showing signs that he was not that primitive. Newport and Smith were forced to travel to Powhatan's home.

The Englishmen's efforts to get Powhatan to kneel to receive his "crown" were useless. At last, with Newport and Smith leaning hard on his shoulders, the tall werowance stooped a bit and the crown was placed on his graying head.[9] When the boats discharged guns—which the English did whenever an important person was honored—Powhatan was terrified. Showing that he understood all too well the significance of all this kneeling, which would symbolically make him a subject of King James of England, Powhatan gave Newport his old moccasins and robe and sent him on his way. Only John Smith knew that "this stately kinde of soliciting made Powhatan so much overvalue himself" that he was contemptuous of the English rather than impressed or grateful. Smith also knew not to put stock in the Indian's word. He believed Indians were "inconstant in everie thing, but what feare constraineth them to keepe."[10]

Smith Gets Back to Work

Despite his opposition to this latest company decision, Smith continued to work to discipline the colonists, grow food, and build. He made the new "gentlemen" settlers part of his lumbering crews. He was, after all, still the head of the colony.

When Newport left for England again in December 1608, once again to get supplies and settlers, the disgraced Ratcliffe went with him. Newport also carried with him a letter to the Virginia Company leaders from Smith:

> When you send againe, I intreate you rather send but thirty Carpenters, husbandmen, gardiners, fisher men, blacksmiths, masons and diggers up of trees, roots, well provided; then a thousand of such as we have; for except wee be able both to lodge them, and feed them, the most will consume with want of necessaries before they can be made good for any thing.[11]

If they wanted to make an immediate profit, Smith explained, they would never get it with "gentlemen."

For the first time since its beginning, Jamestown had a leader who actually led. Smith instilled order among the men by making them perform military drills with arms, and continued to put his crews to work. A well had been dug, which yielded water that was somewhat fresher than the brackish water of the river. As winter approached, corn grown in Jamestown gardens or traded from the Indians was stored.

In the early spring of 1609, Smith was working to complete a second small blockhouse with heavy timbers and holes for shooting guns for defense, across the James River on Hog Island. This area was so-called because it was to house the growing pig population from Jamestown. Smith's work crew included the soldiers garrisoned at Hog Island to watch for any possible Spanish invasion. These men were not used to construction work.

News from Jamestown interrupted Smith's project and sent him back to the fort. Unfortunately, during the winter, rats had come from the ships bringing new colonists. They had multiplied, feasting on half of the settlers' remaining corn supply. The rest of the corn had rotted in storage casks. It is amazing that no one noticed the rats munching on the remaining supply of corn especially since they were said to number in the thousands.[12] Equally mysterious is why the condition of the casks was not checked regularly. Given the colony's past problems, it would have made sense for the settlers to be especially careful with food. Despite Smith's best efforts, however, it seems that he was the only person who took real responsibility for the colony's welfare. Now he would have to think quickly to avoid another famine.

He dealt with the latest crisis by sending groups of colonists away from Jamestown. Some were sent down the James River to live on the oysters that were plentiful in its lower reaches. Another group was sent to Point Comfort to fish, and another toward the falls near modern-day Richmond to hunt and forage. Some settlers left the fort on their own to live among the Indians. By the time the warm weather arrived, the colonists were scattered all along the James River. About eighty out of the two hundred who had been living there when Newport last set sail for England in December 1608 remained in the fort.

Those who had stayed at the fort were a sorry sight when they greeted the next seven ships full of settlers. Smith, despite his energy and practical determination, could not do everything for the colony. He was disgusted with his fellow settlers. He called them "distracted Gluttonous Loyterers," claiming that "had they not beene forced . . . to gather and process such food as could be found, they would all have starved or have eaten one another."[13]

New Arrivals and New Problems

The next boats from England arrived in August 1609, just as the food shortage was giving way to new problems with mosquitoes and bad water. Despite the fresher water from the well they had dug, many settlers were sick with fevers. One of the new ships brought hungry passengers and bad news.

The ship's captain was Samuel Argall, an experienced seaman who was traveling for private investors, not the Virginia Company. He had saved food to trade with the Indians, but seeing the ragged and hungry colonists who met his boat, he gave the food to them instead. Somehow, Ratcliffe, who had been sent from Jamestown in disgrace, had talked the Virginia Company into sending him back with other men who did not like John Smith, Gates, and Archer. They were on Argall's boat, and during the voyage, they had talked to the passengers, as well as to the Virginia Company, trying to turn them against Smith. Overthrowing the Jamestown president was their first order of business.

The Virginia Company had reorganized its corporation. King James signed a new charter on May 23, 1609. The colony had not made an instant profit for investors, and more investors were needed. It must have been obvious even to those far away in England that the government of this new settlement was haphazard at best.

John Smith, the most capable of the original leaders, was the only one who was not a "gentleman" —someone from a well-to-do family. There was no class loyalty toward him from the other leaders. He was also brash and bossy, and because there was no telephone or other fast means of communication, the Virginia Company had no way of knowing the progress Smith had made since he became president at Jamestown. One of the promises the company was making to new investors was that Jamestown's government would be reorganized.

The colony would now be run by a governor, lieutenant-governor, and an admiral. There would be no more council. Already chosen by the company and due to arrive aboard the fleet of nine ships sailing toward Jamestown were Thomas West, Lord De La Warr, governor; Sir Thomas Gates, lieutenant-governor; and Sir George Somers, admiral. These nine ships also carried five hundred new colonists, including women and children.

Five hundred passengers were a lot for nine not-very-big sailing vessels. Plague, a very infectious bacterial disease, spread rapidly. Almost a fifth of the new settlers died even before reaching Virginia. One ship sank, and another was damaged and had to return to England. By the time the remaining seven ships arrived in Jamestown in August, the passengers were so hungry they ran for the fields, eating the corn, still green, that the colonists were trying hard to grow.[14]

Because Lord De La Warr had been delayed in England and did not arrive with the fleet to take charge, Ratcliffe demanded to be seated in his place. John Smith absolutely refused to allow Ratcliffe, Archer, and Martin even to sit on the council. No papers had yet arrived to tell him officially of the change, and Smith held his ground.

The Loss of John Smith

Jamestown's famine conditions were only worsened by the arrival of the new settlers. Parties sent to look for food outside the fort were attacked and killed by American Indians.

John Smith sailed up the James River to the falls, and actually succeeded in buying an American-Indian village there from its chief, Parahunt. It was located on a hill and areas were cleared for planting. But he would not get to carry out his plans to help Jamestown.

Soldiers and frontiersmen of the seventeenth century wore sacks of gunpowder hanging from their belts. While Smith was asleep on his boat one day, a gunpowder explosion set his clothes on fire. He woke up and threw himself overboard to put out the flames. Historians have long debated whether this

John Smith, depicted in this statue, left Jamestown wounded and disappointed, despite his efforts to help the colony succeed.

was an accident or a deliberate attack on Smith. It seems likely that a match was set next to Smith's gunpowder.[15] Smith was, after all, a thorn in the side to many of the petty, inept, yet ambitious men who had arrived to depose him. In any event, Smith was severely burned and in great pain. Realizing that his life was in danger, and knowing he was in no position to fight another attempted assassination, Smith sailed for England.

Smith had been directly responsible for leaving Jamestown with more than fifty houses; had repaired palisades on the fort; created a storehouse to hold provisions and a newly gathered harvest; built a large church, a well, and a blockhouse; increased the livestock populations; and established a fighting force of one hundred trained soldiers. He was also the only man who appreciated the strength and shrewd intelligence of Powhatan and Opechancanough. When Smith left, the Jamestown colonists lost the only real leader they had ever known.

The drive to get more investors for the Virginia Company had resulted in excellent stock sales. Six hundred private investors and fifty-six guilds (groups of craftsmen joined in a sort of union) provided money to help reorganize Jamestown.

This time, there would be leadership. Lord De La Warr was an experienced army officer

THE STARVING TIME

and politician. Sir Thomas Gates and Sir Thomas Dale were experienced soldiers. Gates was to be in command until Lord De La Warr could leave England.

Gates, Captain Christopher Newport, and the admiral of the fleet, Sir George Somers—all rivals for power—sailed aboard the same ship, the *Sea Venture*. The ship was wrecked off Bermuda. The survivors, who included two of the new appointed leaders of Jamestown, were stuck in Bermuda building two more ships for a full year. As a result, the remaining seven-ship fleet that entered Jamestown harbor in August held none of the company's chosen leaders.

The Situation Gets Worse

In Jamestown in late August 1608, the growing season was over and John Smith was severely wounded and had headed home to England. The situation in the settlement quickly went from bad to horrible. With Smith gone, there was no strong leader to organize the new colonists into work crews or military units. "All these latest arrivals could do was eat, and in doing that, they drew down the colony's limited stores," wrote historian Warren M. Billings.[1] The new arrivals were already weakened by disease and months at sea. As winter came on famine took hold.

Powhatan noticed Smith's absence, and took full advantage. Any trip by Jamestown groups to his villages to trade for food was met by angry attacks that seemed to aim at total annihilation of the English settlers. Ratcliffe, who was sent upriver to trade for corn, was tricked by Powhatan and ended up being burned to death. Powhatan then refused to allow any of his people to trade with the colonists. He also declared that any European who left the Jamestown fort for the woods or to fish should be attacked at once. The pigs at Hog Island, destined to see the settlers through the winter, were killed by the Indians. There was no strong English leader like John Smith to challenge the new Indian policy.

The Starving Time Begins

Jamestown now entered the period known to history as the Starving Time. During the terrible winter of 1609–1610, those settlers who were not killed by disease or Indians ate anything they could find, including acorns, horses, rats, and—fulfilling John Smith's earlier

SOURCE DOCUMENT

. . . THERE REMAINED NOT PAST SIXTIE MEN, WOMEN AND CHILDREN, MOST MISERABLE AND POORE CREATURES; AND THOSE WERE PRESERVED FOR THE MOST PART, BY ROOTS, HERBES, ACORNES, WALNUTS, BERRIES, NOW AND THEN A LITTLE FISH . . . EVEN THE SKINNES OF OUR HORSES. . . . [2]

One Jamestown resident wrote this account of the terrible famine conditions during the Starving Time.

bitter prophecy—even each other. One man killed his wife, salted her body, and staved off starvation in this grisly manner (though he was later caught and burned alive for his crime).[3] Tales abounded of people who were so weak that they used their last strength to dig their own graves, lying down to wait for death. When Smith left for England, in the summer of 1608, there were five hundred people living at Jamestown. By the spring of 1610, only sixty colonists remained alive.

Arrival of the *Sea Venture*

While the colonists were suffering, the survivors of the *Sea Venture*, wrecked off Bermuda, were building two ships to carry them on to Jamestown. On board the *Deliverance* and the *Patience* were Sir Thomas Gates, Sir William Somers, and writer William Strachey. Strachey's account of what he saw when he arrived in Jamestown is an important document for historians. (Scholars believe that a copy of Strachey's account of the shipwreck of the *Sea Venture* was the inspiration for Shakespeare's play *The Tempest*.)[4] Also on board the pinnaces were a young widower named John Rolfe, and all but two of the colonists who had shipped out of England on the *Sea Venture* over a year before.

The ships arrived at Jamestown on May 23, 1610. Both survivors and new colonists were shocked at what they saw.[5] The skeletons in rags who stumbled to the shore to greet them must have been a horrifying sight.[6] The fort was torn apart. So were the houses. The wood that had formed the walls had been used for firewood during the winter. So much of the nearby woods had been cleared that venturing any farther to search for wood meant running the risk of attack by lurking Indians. "And it is true, the Indian Killed as fast without, if our men stirred but beyond the bounds of the Blockhouse, as Famine and Pestilence did within," wrote William Strachey.[7]

Evacuation

May was the season for planting, not harvesting. With the Indians refusing to trade for corn, there would be three months with no food to feed over two hundred people. Gates, assessing the food situation, decided to evacuate Jamestown at once. He would take the *Sea Venture* colonists on board their new ships, and the smaller pinnaces—the *Discovery* and *Virginia*—would carry all the Jamestown survivors. The plan was to go north toward Newfoundland. English ships, which often sailed there to fish, could take the survivors home.

Although some of the colonists wanted to set fire to the fort and all the remaining buildings before they left, Gates would not allow it. He ordered the heavy cannons buried, but he took all other arms and any tools worth keeping aboard the ships. At noon on June 7, 1610, guns were fired as a final ritual good-bye, and the four ships headed out. The tide was not with them, and they floated only about five miles, anchoring off Hog Island.

Lord De La Warr Arrives

The next morning, the ships saw a longboat rowing quickly out to meet them. Lord De La Warr had finally arrived in Virginia, with three ships loaded with provisions. At Point Comfort, south of Jamestown, he had been informed that the settlement was being abandoned. He sent his longboat to tell Gates to turn around immediately.

This command may not have been welcomed by many of the survivors, who had lived through the horrifying winter. Lord De La Warr, who knelt in prayer after he stepped ashore at Jamestown, scolded the survivors for laziness in his first speech to them. He promised that the "Starving Time" would not happen again—because punishment for refusing to work would be severe. Like John Smith, De La Warr created work crews and scheduled specific work to be done.

Upon his arrival, Lord De La Warr took firm control of Jamestown. He forced the deserting settlers to return—then forced them back to work.

Some of the first tasks the new governor took on were repairing the church and building a new one. Religion was very important to people of the seventeenth century. Sunday church-going took on great flair and pomp. De La Warr ordered settlers to attend church twice on Sundays and once on Thursdays. Twice

Under Lord De La Warr's power, Jamestown settlers were not only required to perform their share of work around the colony, but also had to attend church on a regular basis.

during the day, all work stopped and prayers were said. If someone missed church once, he or she would be physically punished. The second offense would result in being pilloried in stocks at the center of town. For three times, the settler would have his or her ears cut off.

The fort was repaired, new houses were built, and measures taken to bring in more food. Gates and Newport were sent back to England to tell the Virginia Company not to send any more colonists without also sending a year's supply of food. Samuel Argall, captain of the private ship that landed at Jamestown in 1608, and Somers, who had been appointed the colony's admiral, sailed two ships to Bermuda to bring back food. Unfortunately, these ships were not heard from all summer. In the fall, Argall came back. He had been unable to find Bermuda. Somers did not reappear. He had died in Bermuda, and those who had been aboard his ship had sailed for England.

As usual, trying to get corn from the American Indians by trade or theft was an important project. The Jamestown settlers, under the leadership of George Percy, engaged in some truly disgraceful acts of violence against not only the men, but also the women and children of the tribes of Powhatan's confederacy.[8] This made the Powhatan Indians even more thoroughly disgusted with these Europeans. Now the Powhatan took any chance to kill the white settlers.

The Distracting Search for Gold

Once again, the Virginia Company's desire for gold stopped all work. A Dutchman who had been sent to build a European bed for Powhatan as part of a trading deal, told the governor that there surely was gold in the mountains beyond the upriver falls. De La Warr sent twenty men up the river, hoping to improve a fort already established there to make headquarters for digging expeditions. Once again, vital work at Jamestown was interrupted.

The twenty men of the expedition were invited to a feast by the queen of the Appomattox Indian tribe. After enjoying their meal, all twenty were killed by her warriors. The deaths of these men changed Lord De La Warr's mind about digging in the mountains. However, he did spend some time at the fort. Constant Indian attacks made his stay unpleasant, to say the least. Claiming ill health, he left the men at the fort and returned to Jamestown. In March 1611, he set sail for the West Indies, with fifty colonists, to recover. Instead, after encountering severe weather, he sailed to England.

Despite De La Warr's get-tough policies and the rebuilding he had started in Jamestown, half the colonists had died as usual of disease and malnutrition during the months he spent there. Arriving in England after Gates and Newport, whose news of the Starving Time had thoroughly scared investors, De La Warr's news added to the gloom. Here was the governor, appointed for life, returning from the beleaguered colony after less than a year. Businessmen wondered why they should continue to invest in this losing proposition.

Searching for More Investors

Gates and Newport urged the Virginia Company to try again. They talked about what valuable crops might be grown in the New World and exported back to England. They especially talked about the wonders of Bermuda. The result was that the Virginia Company sought a new charter that would make Virginia include Bermuda.

A company public relations campaign sent a tract to wealthy men all over England. It told of the beauties of this new country and its potential for great wealth. Even Lord De La Warr praised Virginia, in order to help the company. He even said that as soon as his health improved, he would certainly go back.[9]

The fundraising effort was successful. Three ships full of settlers under Sir Thomas Dale, an experienced soldier, set sail from England in the early spring of 1611. Another fleet would leave soon after—six ships under Sir Thomas Gates, who was to be the new lieutenant-governor of Virginia.

Thomas Dale Takes Charge

Dale's ships reached Jamestown on May 19, 1611. Aboard were the first English cows to arrive in the New World, along with goats, dogs, and pigeons.

Dale, whose official title was marshal of Virginia, was not impressed with what he saw.[10] At the small forts defending the mouth of the James River—Forts Henry and Charles—Dale noticed crumbling walls and lazy soldiers who had not even bothered to plant corn. Reaching Jamestown, he found men playing bowling games in the streets, and very little planting begun.

Dale put his own sailors to work planting corn. He also immediately put the Jamestown settlers to work. The men who migrated voluntarily to Virginia seemed to be unable to work on their own, without a strong leader forcing them to do so under threat of punishment. Once again, houses were repaired, wood cut, and work done on the fort, the church, a storehouse, a new stable, a cattle shed, and a blacksmith shop. A brickmaking operation was started, as well as another blockhouse.

Under instructions from the Virginia Company, Dale read out and began implementing a set of laws known as *Lawes Divine, Morall and Martiall*, published by William Strachey in 1612 in England. These laws combined military discipline and civilian laws so that Jamestown's daily affairs would be run like a military organization. All men became soldiers and actually marched to their daily jobs. Stealing was punished by death. Other crimes, such as laziness, not attending church, or speaking out against the colony's leaders, were punished by jail sentences, fines, and hard labor. Settlers who tried to run off to the Indians rather than follow the martial law were hanged, burned, or shot. Indian spies who were captured near the fort were either killed or had a hand cut off as a warning to Powhatan. The efficiency of the settlers improved, and a small corn crop began to grow skyward by the end of May 1611.

A New Settlement

Dale had been instructed to find a replacement site for Jamestown Island that would be healthier, better defended against the always-feared Spanish, and closer to the still-hoped-for route to China. The American Indians, who were beginning to be outnumbered by the continuing arrival of new white settlers, were not to be offered bargains. They were only to be pushed aside by whatever means necessary. Instead of the outdated armor that had been sent with the earlier settlers, Dale arrived with full upper-body armor, which was able to defend against arrows much more effectively.

Dale sailed upriver by boat, and three hundred fifty heavily armed soldiers marched overland toward the falls, located near present-day Richmond, Virginia. On the way, the men on foot were attacked several times by Indians. One of the attacking tribes was led by a werowance known to the English as Jack of the Feather. This expert leader inspired courage in his soldiers by covering himself with feathers and swan's wings and claiming to be immune to English bullets.

The site Dale chose was high ground in a bend of the river, about twenty miles south of the falls, at a place now called Curles Neck. Dale named it Henricopolis, which was soon shortened to Henrico, in honor of Henry, Prince of Wales. According to historian James Axtell, "They built Henrico on a defensible neck of land and paled [fenced] it like an English town in colonial Ireland."[11] There were about nine acres of open fields with fresh water springs. Blockhouses, storehouses, a church, and houses with brick first floors were built with great speed. A moat was dug to protect against Indian attacks. By the time Governor Sir Thomas Gates arrived in late summer of 1611 with six ships, more arms, tools, food, soldiers, and more settlers, the Starving Time was officially over.

Jamestown, however, was not abandoned. The original settlement was maintained even as Henrico developed into a strong English colony.

New settlements sprang up along the James River, largely through the confiscation or burning of Indian cornfields and villages. Through absolute adherence to the tough martial laws, the English colonists slowly became disciplined members of a community. The Indians, seeing their land disappear and their fighting men outnumbered, retreated farther inland, although they continued to make attacks on the new English forts. Powhatan moved the capital of his empire to the Orapak village at the head of the Chickahominy River.

JOHN ROLFE AND TOBACCO

Englishman John Rolfe, a twenty-eight-year-old widower, began experimenting with growing West Indies tobacco at Jamestown in the spring of 1612. Tobacco, whether smoked or chewed, had become very popular in England. The settlers at Jamestown often smoked American-Indian tobacco, but it was hard to sell to the English, who disliked its bitter taste.

The Search for Food Continues

In the spring of 1612, even though the winter had not been disastrous as in years past, food was again a problem. George Percy, who had been left in charge of Jamestown several times, surprised the colony by sailing a pinnace on which he had been sent to catch fish, straight back to England with his catch. Passing him came a ship called the *Treasurer*, captained by Samuel Argall. It was well outfitted for attack, with fourteen cannons. Argall was dispatched by Gates to sail up the James, shoot the cannon at American Indian villages, and then go in and take their corn. It was on one of these corn-stealing trips in the spring of 1613, that Argall came up with his plan to kidnap Pocahontas.

The Pocahontas Plot

Capturing American-Indian children and priests and converting them to Christianity was one of the directives the Virginia Company had given Lord De La Warr as early as 1609. Capturing Pocahontas, who had not visited Jamestown since her friend Captain John Smith had sailed away in the fall of 1608, would accomplish several things. One would be the conversion of a young woman who already liked the English, and the other would be to have a hostage who would get Powhatan's attention. Powhatan would most likely be willing to bargain—to give the English back some of their guns and swords and lots of corn—for his beloved daughter.

Now around sixteen years old, Pocahontas had been sent by her father to visit the Patawomeke Indians, who were part of the Powhatan confederacy, as a corn agent. The Patawomeke chief, Iapazaws, was bribed by Argall to bring his wife and Pocahontas down the riverbank to Argall's ship, and go aboard to visit. The trio remained on board all night. The next morning, when Pocahontas became suspicious, Iapazaws and his wife left the ship. Argall then set sail with the Indian princess as his prisoner. A message was sent to Powhatan that his daughter "could be ransomed in exchange for all English prisoners and runaways currently in his hands, as well as for all the captured or stolen weapons and tools, plus, of course, large quantities of corn."[1]

A Wedding

Powhatan agreed to the ransom demand, but then failed to send what the English wanted. It was nine months before the English heard from Powhatan again. By then, Pocahontas had received instruction in Christianity, renounced her Indian religion, and been baptized under the name Rebecca. She "accused [her father] . . . of loving a bunch of old swords, guns and axes better than her."[2]

Then, Pocahontas married English settler John Rolfe in the Jamestown church, on April 5, 1614. She was given away by an uncle. Powhatan was still smart enough to know it was dangerous for him to enter Jamestown.

The father of the bride, however, sent two dressed deerskins to the wedding, and vowed to encourage all his tribes to have peaceful relations with the English.

Powhatan ruled over an empire of many American-Indian villages.

When an English peace delegation asked Powhatan to allow another of his daughters to marry Sir Thomas Dale, Powhatan said that giving up one daughter to the English was quite enough. He urged the English to stop the speeches about it before he became irritated.[3]

The Chickahominy Indians, not part of Powhatan's empire, also promised peace with the Europeans. For the first time in seven years, there was a truce between English and Indians.

Dale began a new policy of encouraging private property. Individually owned plantations soon sprang up in the Tidewater area.

John Rolfe, meanwhile, had continued to experiment with tobacco. When he and his new Indian bride settled at Henrico, he began to grow tobacco on large, cultivated fields and worked at learning to cure it to travel safely aboard ships bound for England.

Tobacco

The English had not found the gold they believed Virginia held, but tobacco soon became its substitute. Tobacco was very popular in England, although many people opposed its use strongly. In fact, no less a personage than King James I released a tract condemning tobacco. He said it came from the barbarous, godless Indians, and that smoking was "a custome lothsome to the eye, hateful to the Nose, harmefull to the braine, dangerous to the Lungs."[4] Later medical discoveries would prove him right, but in the seventeenth century, few people listened to his warnings. At last, the Jamestown settlers had found a commodity that would make the settlement profitable for its investors.

Sir Thomas Dale, who was again governing Jamestown after Gates's departure, tried to control how much tobacco was being grown. He believed that agriculture, particularly the growing of corn, should be rotated on various plots of land, and the tasks of growing different crops distributed among all the settlers.

Dale, whose stern organization and genius for expanding land areas for colonization had resulted in stability for Jamestown, finally got tired of fighting the still-high death rate among the settlers. Mosquitoes, bad water, and poor nutrition were still taking a terrible toll. The constant shortage of colonists made it hard to keep expanding the English settlements beyond the falls.

Pocahontas Goes to England

Dale left for England in May 1616. John Rolfe, Pocahontas, their new son, Thomas, and about a dozen American Indians went with him. Rolfe wrote an account of the settlement to take back to England. Living at the English settlements of Jamestown, Kecoughtan, Henrico, Bermuda Nether, and Dales-Gift there were a total of 351 people. Of these, 205 were officers and laborers, including tradesmen, such as blacksmiths, coopers, glassmakers, and tanners, and indentured servants. There were 81 farmers, and 65 women and children. There was adequate livestock, and crops were being planted. Despite Rolfe's boastful tone, this was not a large number of people, even in one place. It was a good thing the Indians were at peace.

Pocahontas became a curiosity of English society for the nine months that she was in England. While there, she had at least one meeting with her old friend John Smith.

London was not the healthiest city, especially in the winter, and Pocahontas was as unused to the English air as the English were to the Virginia climate. She became ill, probably with the lung disease tuberculosis.[5] Sadly, Pocahontas died before the ship that was to carry the Rolfe family back to Virginia had even left English waters. The ship turned around and Pocahontas was buried at Gravesend, England.

The Rolfes' son, Thomas, had also fallen sick. John Rolfe left him behind to recover under the

Sadly, Pocahontas died during her visit to England, far from her homeland.

care of Sir Lewis Stukley. Rolfe then set sail for Virginia. Although John Rolfe never saw his son again, Thomas Rolfe did travel back to Virginia years later. He farmed and had a family of his own.

Cultivating the Cash Crop

After Dale's return to England, the government of Jamestown had been taken over by Captain George Yeardley. Like John Rolfe, Yeardley believed tobacco was the cash crop the colony desperately needed. He encouraged settlers to cultivate tobacco wherever they could. In addition, a new company policy that gave stockholders and servants grants of land when their indenture was done changed the distribution of property. Private investors sponsored settlers by offering large tracts of land, or plantations, along the banks of the James River.

These new colonists were spread up and down the river, unprotected from Indian attack. When Samuel

SOURCE DOCUMENT

THERE IS AN HERBE WHICH IS SOWED APART BY ITSELFE . . .
THE SPANYARDS GENERALLY CALL IT TABACCO. THE
LEAVES THEREOF BEING DRIED AND BROUGHT INTO
POUDER, THEY USE TO TAKE THE FUME OR SMOKE THEREOF,
BY SUCKING IT THOROW PIPES MADE OF CLAY, INTO THEIR
STOMACKE AND HEAD; FROM WHENCE IT PURGETH
SUPERFLUOUS FLEAME [PHLEGM] AND OTHER GROSSE
HUMOURS, AND OPENETH ALL THE PORES AND PASSAGES OF
THE BODY . . . [6]

Thomas Heriot, a member of the expedition to colonize Roanoke Island, wrote this account of the supposedly good uses of Virginia tobacco.

Argall replaced Yeardley as deputy governor in 1617, the undisciplined colonists had once again stopped growing corn in their drive to make money from tobacco, which was being grown even in the streets of Jamestown itself.

Argall put the martial law that had been allowed to slip when Dale sailed to England back into effect. He decreed that two acres of corn had to be planted for every one acre of tobacco, and that any settler who taught an American Indian to shoot a rifle would be shot himself.

Natural disasters—such as a hailstorm that damaged crops and an unusual summer drought—made 1618 a troublesome year. Added to these problems was the fact that despite Argall's gift for strict governance, he was not especially honest. When he was caught selling servants and livestock privately, and not for the benefit of the Virginia Company, Lord De La Warr hurried his plans to return to Virginia. He left England on a ship with two hundred settlers, many of whom died along the way. The dead included Lord De La Warr himself. In his place, George Yeardley returned to become governor.

The Great Charter

The Virginia Company was disgusted with the lack of return on its investment. By now, however, the company had invested so much that it would lose even more money if it pulled out of Jamestown. The company decided to make one more try.

Sir Edwin Sandys, who replaced Sir Thomas Smythe as head of the Virginia Company, thought the colony would never prosper if a traditional English society were not begun and maintained. Martial law had been needed at one time, but that time had passed. Sandys instructed Yeardley to replace *Lawes Divine, Morall and Martiall* with rules based on English common law. These were called the Great Charter.

On July 30, 1619, a meeting was held in the church at Jamestown, to elect twenty-two burgesses (representatives). These men would swear allegiance to the English Crown. This was the first General Assembly in Virginia, and is now the oldest republican government in the world. It began passing laws about relations with American Indians, the treatment of indentured servants, and tobacco pricing. It also

SOURCE DOCUMENT

V. WHEREAS IN ALL OTHER THINGS, WE REQUIRE THE SAID GENERAL ASSEMBLY, AS ALSO THE SAID COUNCIL OF STATE, TO IMITATE AND FOLLOW THE POLICY OF THE FORM OF GOVERNMENT—LAWS, CUSTOMS, AND MANNER OF TRIAL, AND OTHER ADMINISTRATION OF JUSTICE, USED IN THE REALM OF *ENGLAND*, AS NEAR AS MAY BE, EVEN AS OURSELVES, BY HIS MAJESTY'S LETTERS PATENT, ARE REQUIRED. [7]

This 1621 ordinance directs the Virginia General Assembly to follow the laws of England in locally governing the colony.

looked at individual criminal offenses. Since it was the middle of a hot summer, the Assembly's first session was only four days long. However, it marked a beginning for representative government in the colony.

Sandys continued to send a stream of new settlers, including single women, and provisions for the colony. More than three thousand settlers arrived in Virginia between 1619 and 1622. A group of ninety young women arrived in 1619. Each male settler who married one of these eligible young "maids" had to pay her passage with "one hundred and fiftie pounds of the best leafe tobacco." The practice of sending young women to marry the bachelors in the colony continued. Stable families were also sent to Virginia, as well as young orphans. In addition, more attention was being paid to ensuring that men specifically skilled in crafts and farming were sent to Virginia.

The Start of American Slavery

Another shipment of people during this period was to have lasting consequences for Virginia and what would later become the United States. In late August 1619, a Portuguese slave ship docked at Jamestown. The captain, in need of supplies, sold twenty Africans there. At that time, the Africans were treated as indentured servants, who could work out their time and be given grants of land, just as white indentured servants were entitled to do. This would change dramatically in 1661, when the practice of African slavery became an institution.

Sandys continued to encourage large land grants and the kind of private enterprise that led to plantations and more tobacco cultivation. Unfortunately, since tobacco could only be grown in one place for about three years before the nutrients of the soil were depleted, this meant constantly finding new fields to cultivate. The settlers, now scattered throughout the Tidewater section of Virginia, once again eyed the cleared fields that belonged to the American Indians. Trouble was bound to erupt.

9

A NEW WEROWANCE MAKES PLANS

The powerful werowance Powhatan died of old age in 1618. Itopatin, Powhatan's brother, became the new werowance of the now depleted Powhatan empire. By 1619, the older and much more powerful Opechancanough had replaced Itopatin.

At first, Opechancanough declared and showed great friendship toward the English. He even accepted a visit from Captain George Thorpe, a gentleman who planned, at the request of the Virginia Company, to start a school for American Indians. The company hoped that the "savage" Indians would voluntarily send their children to be educated out of their "heathen" ways at this school. Thorpe even built Opechancanough a house, with a door that locked. This seasoned, strong, and crafty Indian soldier delighted in going in and out, locking the door before and behind, many times a day.[1] The Indians, however, were reluctant to send their children to Thorpe's school. They were afraid the children might be held as hostages to help the English bargain for American-Indian land and corn.

The Reign of Opechancanough

Sir Thomas Yeardley, who was suffering ill health, was succeeded in 1621 by Sir Francis Wyatt, a relative of Sir Edwin Sandys by marriage. Wyatt arrived in Virginia with a document declaring free government in the colonies. Wyatt's reforms included quarterly sessions of the court. He also regularly assembled the legislature to rule on local matters. John Rolfe, who had remarried, became secretary of the colony.

Wyatt hoped that peace with the American Indians would continue. Daily relations with the Indians, who seemed almost like neighbors to many of the colonists, had been friendly recently. But Opechancanough resented the contempt that the English barely hid for his people and their ways. It was apparent that the ever-growing European settlements, which offered friendship only if the Indians would become Christians, were "a menace to their existence as a race of free people."[2] To retreat west would mean losing their empire and facing new conflicts with other tribes. To make peace meant losing more and more land to the Europeans.

Opechancanough was fierce and proud, and was an excellent political strategist. He had shown what he thought of converting to European ways in his youth, when he went right back to American-Indian customs after spending his youth in Spain and Mexico.

Opechancanough felt the logical answer to stopping the disrespect being shown to his people was an all-out surprise attack on the increasingly scattered English settlements.

The burial of a high ruler such as Powhatan carried with it as much pomp and ceremony, Algonquian Indian style, as that of any European king. Preparations for the funeral took a very long time. In fact, rumor reached Jamestown that the "taking up of Powhatan's bones," in 1621, was supposed to be the cue for the Indians to rise up and destroy the English.[3] Opechancanough hotly denied this, but Governor Yeardley warned the men of the English plantations to be alert. When nothing occurred after the funeral, the plantation owners relaxed, and the Indians continued to move freely in and out of the plantations.

Jack of the Feather

Enter Jack of the Feather, whose real name was Nemattanow. The English population, still facing high death rates every year, numbered around thirteen hundred by 1622. More and more individual new-comers, who were not part of the Virginia Company, were constantly challenging American-Indian terri-tory. Jack of the Feather fought against these incursions, still claiming to be invincible against English bullets. But, of course, he was not. He killed a planter named Morgan, and then, legend has it, re-turned to Morgan's farm wearing the English planter's cap. He boasted of the murder to two servants, who shot him. They then put the wounded Indian into a boat and rowed him eight miles to see Sir Francis Wyatt, by then governor of Jamestown. Jack of the Feather, fearing that his death would demoralize his tribe, asked two things before he died: that it not be told he had died from a bullet wound, and that he be buried among the English.[4]

Hearing of Jack of the Feather's death, Opechancanough reacted with threats of revenge. He took them back, however, when Wyatt reacted with equal threats. The great werowance backed down, renewing his vows of peaceful coexistence with the English.

A Powhatan-Indian Attack

Two weeks later, on March 22, 1622, at exactly 8:00 A.M., all the Indians of the Powhatan empire, acting on orders from Opechancanough, sprang up to commit a massacre that would take 347 English lives. In homes, in fields, sitting at breakfast, or tilling the fields, the English lost their lives to Indian tomahawks. Among the dead was John Rolfe (although some sources say he was already ill and did not die in the massacre).[5] Also dead was George Thorpe, who had hoped to convert American Indians to Christianity. New industries, such as iron foundries and glassmaking projects, lost all their artisans. Buildings and machinery were destroyed. All the plantations upriver were burned, and most of the residents killed.

Jamestown, although beleaguered by disease, laziness, and bad management from its beginning, survived the massacre. An American-Indian servant, who had been raised like the son of a planter, had told his master, Richard Pace, that all the English were to be murdered the next morning. Pace quickly rowed downstream and across the river to Jamestown, alerting the fort. There was enough time to warn a few nearby plantations, whose settlers also escaped the attack. Not expecting armed resistance, the warriors assigned to attack Jamestown sped homeward.

One third of the settlers in the expanded Jamestown, however, had died. New enterprises came to a halt. The survivors of outlying plantations scurried to settlements with forts.

After a month spent recovering from the attack, Governor Wyatt's troops set out for total revenge. When they failed to find the elusive Indians, they burned their cornfields and their villages. Between 1622 and 1624, the English did their best to search and destroy.

The Company Gives Up

Thoroughly disgusted with the misadventures of their poor investment, the stockholders of the Virginia Company attacked its current director, Edwin Sandys. They claimed he had sent huge numbers of settlers into Virginia and offered tracts of land, but did not bring additional troops to counter American-Indian attacks and had made only a tiny profit. King James, now tired of the whole affair, sued the company and took away its charter.

But Virginia, and all its settlements, still existed, and the question remained: What was to be done? As this was being decided, King James died on March 27, 1625. James's son, Charles I, had an answer. Virginia was proclaimed a royal colony. Because Jamestown was the first settlement, it became the first capital of Virginia.

A royal governor, personally appointed by the king, would preside over the colony. To the Powhatan, however, who had been hunted down ruthlessly by the English since the 1622 uprising, who governed was not important. What was important was trying to preserve their culture and whatever land they could. Opechancanough offered peace in 1632. This uneasy, bitter peace would remain until 1644.

10

JAMESTOWN SETTLES DOWN

From its hopeful but impractical beginnings in 1607, the new Jamestown, capital of the royal colony of Virginia in 1625, became less of a village than a springboard for other settlements. It also became the center of James River trade. As the capital of the colony, it was home to the courts and legislature. Although land for growing tobacco, which rapidly depleted the soil, was scarce in Jamestown, tobacco business dealings were centered in the capital.

First fleeing to Jamestown from outlying plantations after the 1622 Indian attack, old and new settlers soon spread out to new plantations throughout the Tidewater region of Virginia. Fields exhausted by tobacco began to be cultivated for wheat and flax. This was a practical measure, but it left planters still needing more land to grow the soil-depleting tobacco.

The Colony Grows

King Charles I wanted the settlers at Jamestown to agree to sell their tobacco only to England. But the Virginia planters were no longer hungry, and they had

These ruins of shops are a reminder of the bustling town Jamestown once was.

learned to appreciate the independence and freedom that owning large tracts of river-front land afforded them.

By 1634, the population of settlers had doubled from the twelve hundred in 1622. Enough corn was being grown to feed all the colonists, and five thousand bushels of corn were shipped to Plymouth Colony in Massachusetts. (This first New England colony had been started by English Separatists, who had left England in search of religious freedom, in 1620.) Tobacco exports to Europe continued.

Jamestown became important as a learning ground for self-government. In the 1600s, freedom of speech was unheard of, and any diversion from the religious beliefs of the official Church of England was not tolerated. Only men who owned property could vote. Ruling families in England also produced the rulers for the New World. This had been a great problem for John Smith, the first talented manager of Jamestown, because he was the son of a farmer, not a nobleman. The settlers of the New World, planted in Virginia, no longer starving, began to test these old assumptions about government, religion, and social class.

The next important governor at Jamestown was Sir William Berkeley. He arrived in 1642, replacing John Harvey, who had become governor in 1628. Harvey had fought with the members of the Virginia Council of State, had made a tentative peace with the Indians, and helped settlers in the new colony of Maryland. Because the Jamestown colonists considered Maryland a Catholic colony, this did not make Harvey popular.

Sir William Berkeley began his thirty-five-year governorship of the royal colony of Virginia in 1642. Berkeley was a charming and courteous man, but he could be ruthless to his enemies. Like many of the men who would rule in Virginia, he was the younger son of prominent family, which meant he had not inherited the land or rank of the older sons of his family. Because they had connections with the Crown, however, many younger sons were able to seek their fortunes as leaders in the American colonies.

Berkeley began a large plantation and governed Virginia during the years the General Assembly was working its way into government, American-style. He encouraged a parliamentary (legislative) system with a division of power between geographical factions. He encouraged an English way of life in the colonies. Under his tenure, a new brick church was built at Jamestown to celebrate the only acceptable religion, the Church of England. All along the James River there were new docks and boats moved from plantation to plantation. Berkeley also encouraged the growth of colonial independence, which went along with the growth of the colonies. This weakened his own and England's position in Virginia, however.

The English Civil War and Jamestown

Troubles in England between Charles I and Parliament in the 1640s resulted in civil war in England. Charles, who had fled London, wanted to make sure that the colony of Virginia remained with the Crown. Although some factions wanted the Virginia Company to be revived, Berkeley was opposed to this. Virginia remained a royal colony.

Jamestown had expanded greatly. The town now had busy streets. While the houses of poorer residents were wattle-and-daub, more prosperous inhabitants lived in frame houses or even two-story brick manors. Potters, glassmakers, jewelers, coopers (barrel makers),

Jamestown became a thriving city that was home to many kinds of artisans. Here, a modern re-enactor shows how glass blowing was done at the Jamestown settlement.

carpenters, winemakers, and weavers were among the many craftsmen at Jamestown. The impressive brick church was the center of town, and a whole section, called New Town, the upscale residential section, expanded beyond the fort.

All up and down the river, plantations were thriving. The "seasoning" of new settlers, where most died within the first year, had not yet stopped completely, mainly because the connection between mosquitoes and disease was not understood. But wells had stopped the diseases caused by contaminated water, and starvation had been ended by efficient planting of crops, particularly corn, and a constant stream of new supplies aboard ships packed with settlers. English town life, with fine china and silk clothing, was beginning to take hold at the plantations and wealthier homes in Jamestown.

Opechancanough Returns

All seemed to be going smoothly until, on April 18, 1644, Opechancanough struck again. The colonists were spreading out across the Tidewater region, planting crops in ever-expanding fields. The Indians were being forced into small corners of their former territory. Opechancanough, who was over ninety years old in 1644, knew what was happening and was determined to make one last stand.

After Opechancanough had made peace with the English in 1632, the colonists had relaxed their guard against Indian attack. Powhatan's tribes were pushed westward until they were no longer even able to take advantage of trade with the English colony. Most Indian trading was done now with tribes near the Potomac and Susquehanna rivers that flowed into the Chesapeake Bay, and with the Occaneechi people on the Roanoke River.

Although the white population of Virginia by 1644 was around ten thousand, Opechancanough was well aware of the divisions of loyalty caused by the civil war in England. He reasoned that aid from England would not be likely and that a surprise attack would discourage further expansion and help him win back some of his lands.[1]

Rising swiftly and decisively, Opechancanough's warriors killed nearly five hundred English settlers. People fled to safety at fortified settlements, but most planters were able to return to their own lands within six months. Once again, Jamestown was not destroyed.

Berkeley gathered an army and pursued the Powhatan tribes. Fighting between English and Powhatan Indians continued for two years. It ended only in 1646 when Opechancanough was captured.

Old and frail and able to see only with his eyelids propped open, this intelligent and fearless werowance was carried into Jamestown on a litter (stretcher). He was put in prison, where crowds of curious Englishmen came to stare at him. Opechancanough indignantly called for the governor. He complained, saying that "had it been his Fortune to take Sir William Berkeley Prisoner, he should not meanly have exposed him as a Show to the People."[2]

Berkeley had planned to ship Opechancanough to England as a present to King Charles I. According to historian Ivor Hume,

> Mercifully, in that the Indian patriarch was spared the voyage and the subsequent humiliation, the James Towne English proved so ill-disciplined that they could not protect their prisoner from themselves. Unable to see or to recognize his danger, the defenseless old man died at the hands of a soldier who boldly shot him in the back.[3]

So ended an era and an empire.

JAMESTOWN MOVES ON

With the threat from the scattered and leaderless Powhatan people forever silenced, Virginia continued to prosper. Governor Berkeley himself lived on a plantation of a thousand acres. He worked on innovations in agriculture, and his plantation included an array of artisans, and an orchard of fifteen hundred trees.

A New Government for England

The continuing civil war in England between those loyal to King Charles I, called Royalists, and those who were offended that their monarch had bypassed Parliament to make laws, called Parliamentarians, Puritans, or Roundheads, because of the way they wore their hair, seemed remote to the daily lives of the planters spread along the James River. Berkeley and the General Assembly, however, were loyal to the Crown. When Charles I was beheaded in 1649, the colony was shocked. They were left to wonder what would happen to them now.

Oliver Cromwell, a Puritan and a powerful political strategist, declared England a commonwealth—a

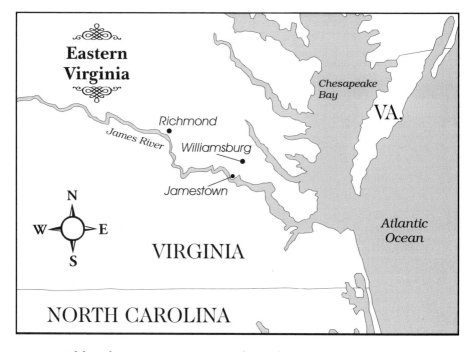

Although Jamestown remained as the seventeenth century went on, other cities including Richmond and Williamsburg became more prominent. This map of present-day Virginia shows where the cities are in relation to each other.

nation founded on law, with a head of state, but whose authority rested with the people—in 1649. Just because he declared the commonwealth, however, did not mean that the Royalists would agree. Civil war still raged.

Berkeley favored the Royalists, and he and the General Assembly wanted Charles I's son, Charles II, to become king of England. Many Royalists, called Cavaliers, fled to Virginia to avoid death at the hand of Cromwell's Roundheads. It was not until 1652 that

Cromwell got around to sending a fleet of ships to Virginia. Commissioners were to set up a new form of government for the colony. Colonists were armed and cannons were ready when one of these English ships sailed into Jamestown.

A New Government for Virginia

Many of the commissioners had spent time in Virginia and the colonists recognized them. The only real change they proposed to make was in the governorship. Berkeley resigned, and the General Assembly appointed Richard Bennet, a Roundhead who had fled to Maryland during the reign of Charles I, to be its governor.

During the commonwealth period, Jamestown enjoyed a liberal rule, and the General Assembly continued to expand its legislative rights. Refining English law to fit the circumstances of colonial society began a breakdown of rigid traditions. Many of the assemblymen were merchants, not lawyers. They looked at laws from a practical standpoint. This tendency toward reform and toward creating law to fit specific circumstances worked well for Virginia in most cases. However, according to historian Warren M. Billings, "Their quest for power inclined them to experimentation, and they measured results against a standard of utility. . . . Results, such as indentured servitude and chattel slavery, could be perversely clever adaptations whose effects have lasted for centuries."[1] Also, because laws made for the public good often favored monetary self-interest, planters spread along the James River were less than pleased to be excluded from important legislative sessions. This would lead to problems among the colonists.

The Return of the Royalists

Commonwealth rule in Jamestown lasted only eight years. When Charles II, son of Charles I, became king of England in 1660 and the Royalists returned to power, the new king demanded that tobacco and other trade goods from the Virginia plantations be shipped only to England. Customs duties—fees charged when a product entered a new port—would even apply to products sent from one colony to another, as if the items were going to a foreign country.

Berkeley, renamed governor, was angered at Charles II's stance, particularly in regard to taxes and building in Jamestown. Charles II wanted to dictate how many buildings would be erected, what kind would be built, and put taxes on any new structures.

Jamestown was still predominantly populated by young, single men. New immigrants tended to go to outlying plantations instead of staying in what was then called James Cittie.[2] Half of the people living in Jamestown were indentured servants. A small number of these were Africans, usually brought to Jamestown from the West Indies. The town was separated into industrial zones because of the large number of craftsmen. Brew masters—men who made beer and other alcoholic beverages—flourished, as did taverns. By the 1660s, the town was becoming rigidly divided according to wealth.

Problems Continue

Once again, weather conditions took a great toll on Virginia. In 1667, a hailstorm dropping pieces of ice as big as a fist destroyed property and livestock. Then it rained for forty days straight, right after Dutch ships, at war with England, came up the James River and captured a number of English ships.

Tobacco prices fell as a result of the war with the Dutch. Governor Berkeley wanted to diversify Virginia's economy by growing cash crops other than tobacco. He persuaded King Charles II to provide funds to experiment with new crops. Tobacco planters, however, felt threatened. They feared they would get less money for their tobacco crops. Berkeley became angry at those who withheld support, and he pushed for legislation anyway. As Berkeley got older, he came to trust only his inner circle of friends, and filled all political vacancies with people who agreed with him. This made it difficult for representative government to flourish through the General Assembly. These problems, coupled with Charles II's giving permission to several members of the royal family to sell land grants in the growing territory, and a disease among the colony's cattle in 1672, caused great unrest among the settlers. Jamestown and the surrounding area had around forty thousand people at that time. Men who owned horses numbered eight thousand, there were six thousand white servants and two thousand African slaves. Virginia's way of dealing with slavery would become the guideline for all other

William Berkeley was, for a while, an effective governor of the Virginia colony.

American colonies. This would eventually have terrible ramifications for what would become the United States.

Bacon's Rebellion

When the Susquehannock Indians struck near present-day Richmond, an alarm spread among the planters.

Governor Berkeley refused to grant permission for the assembled planters to follow and attack the Susquehannock. Other bands of American Indians continued the harassing attacks.

One of the plantations attacked belonged to Nathaniel Bacon, Jr., a young English gentleman who had only been in the colony since 1674 and was a member of the Council of State. During the attack, his overseer and a servant were killed. Angered by Governor Berkeley's refusal to support a revenge attack on the American Indians, Bacon took command of a group of sixty men who rode into the forest and killed many of the Occaneechi. These Indians had been considered friendly, and Berkeley was furious.[3]

Bacon, with forty armed rebels, sailed down the James River to take his seat in the new Grand Assembly, hastily convened by Berkeley. When Bacon arrived to take his seat in the assembly as a representative of Henrico, town gunners fired cannons at his party under orders from Berkeley. They were forced to flee upriver. Bacon slipped back into Jamestown under cover of darkness and met with influential men who were tired of Berkeley and his increasing influence over a small group of councilors.

The result was that Bacon, with the backing of powerful men in Jamestown, raised an army of one thousand and returned to Jamestown. With this show of strength, he was able to get permission from the General Assembly to fight the American Indians on a larger scale.

Berkeley declared Bacon a rebel against his government. At Middle Plantation, which would later become the city of Williamsburg, Bacon gathered his forces. He held a public meeting at which he declared defiance of the colonial government and any reinforcements sent from England by the king. Bacon demanded that the British Parliament hear his case against Berkeley. This demand constituted armed rebellion against the Crown.

Bacon's army fought the Appomattox tribe, following them into the forest near present-day Petersburg, Virginia. Then his army turned downstream to Jamestown. The men burned the town, and destroyed the new statehouse and brick church. Governor Berkeley escaped to the eastern shore of the James River. Before Bacon could complete his plans to chase Berkeley, he fell ill with fever and dysentery, all too familiar to Jamestown. He died on October 26, 1676.

Left without a leader, Bacon's army dissolved. Berkeley came back to power, hanging twenty-three of Bacon's followers. Tensions within the colony had become so great that King Charles II recalled Berkeley to England. He died within a year.

The Shift to Williamsburg

Jamestown never fully recovered from Bacon's attack. Jamestown's history shifted to Virginia as a whole, and particularly to Middle Plantation, which would soon be called Williamsburg. Though a series of governors came to Virginia, and Jamestown was still called the capital, Williamsburg became the colony's real focal point. Very few people still lived in Jamestown by 1698, when a disastrous fire reduced the town to "a heap of bricks and rubbish," according to historian Virgil Jones.[4]

With Jamestown still an unhealthy place to live, the General Assembly decided that a new statehouse should be built at Middle Plantation. A college, William and Mary, had already been established there. Governor Francis Nicholson proposed that the colonial capital be moved there, and its name changed to Williamsburg, in honor of King William III.

Although it still held several plantations, Jamestown reverted to swamp and wilderness. What is truly amazing about this unhealthy, swamp spot on the James River that consumed so many lives is that it had succeeded at all. Settlers, driven by hopes of riches and freedom, kept arriving on ships that were themselves unhealthy and dangerous. The sheer numbers of people, willing to live and die against all odds, finally beat the mosquitoes, brackish water, hostile Indians, and their own lack of preparation for the rigors of settling in such a spot.

·12·

JAMESTOWN REVISITED

Today, visitors to Jamestown arrive over a road built across one of the many tidal water passages of the James River. Only one original tower of brick from the seventeenth century still stands. A few reconstructions include a brick church, monuments, and signposts. There are many long trenches from archaeological digs to discover the dimensions of the original fort and artifacts to learn about the lives of the people who lived and died in Jamestown.

Much has been discovered about Jamestown in recent years that continually changes assumptions about the people and buildings of the early settlement. It was recently discovered that both the *Discovery* and the *Godspeed*, two of the first three boats to arrive at Jamestown harbor, were about one third bigger than formerly believed. These ships have been reconstructed, and can be visited. The Jamestown fort, long thought to have been partially buried in the naturally changing shore of the river, has been discovered entirely on land at the original settlement. Dedicated archaeologists are still discovering items within the fort area that fill in the gaps in knowledge about Jamestown.

Today, archaeologists make digs at Jamestown to learn more about how the settlers lived. Here, the site of a dig is covered to protect it from the weather.

The property of the original settlement now houses a functioning glassworks, a museum, and a bookstore. Enthusiastic and informed members of the Association for the Preservation of Virginia Antiquities run tours and answer questions about the history of the settlement and about the archaeological developments.

Just before crossing the road to Jamestown, the modern visitor to America's first permanent settlement can choose instead to go to Jamestown Settlement, a living-history reconstruction that contains a museum, a reconstructed fort, and a reconstruction of the Powhatan village that meant both life and death to the first English settlers. Staff members of the

At a reconstructed Powhatan village, visitors can view native houses like those that existed at the time the first European settlers arrived at Jamestown.

Jamestown-Yorktown Foundation dress in period costumes and engage in typical seventeenth-century tasks of both American-Indian and English populations. Tour guides explain what visitors are seeing and fill them in on the larger history of the area. Children are encouraged to dress in costumes, and engage in some of the English and American-Indian activities of the time.

The reconstructed fort contains wattle-and-daub houses, a wooden church, blacksmith shops, and armories. From the doors of the fort, one can view the reconstructions of the *Susan Constant, Godspeed,* and *Discovery,* and then walk down to the water to board them. The museum takes the visitor from the beginning

Today, this monument to the Jamestown settlers stands as a reminder of the great dangers the first Englishmen in the New World faced to build their colony.

These are reproductions of settlers' houses at Jamestown today.

of Jamestown in 1607 to the movement of the capital to Williamsburg in 1699.

Visitors can take a ferry across the James River, with or without their cars. Viewing the area as the first English settlers must have done, from the calm and wide river, is a special treat. It is easy to see why these weary travelers, unaware of the perils of this swampy land, would have wanted to anchor near the inviting shores of this river, in a harbor that seemed to usher them into a safe, comfortable home in a New World.

★ TIMELINE ★

1607—*May 13*: One hundred four settlers land at Jamestown, after traveling five months from Blackwall, England; They were sent by the Virginia Company of London.

December 19: After being held prisoner, Captain John Smith meets Powhatan, ruler of a native empire; Powhatan's daughter Pocahontas saves Smith's life. During the winter, many settlers die.

1609—John Smith is wounded and returns to England; The winter is dubbed the Starving Time.

1610—Sir Thomas Gates arrives with settlers, realizes there is no food, and departs for England with remaining colonists and new arrivals; Thomas West, Lord De La Warr, arriving with supply ships, encourages the departing colonists to return.

1612—Sir Thomas Dale institutes the *Lawes Divine, Morall and Martiall* and enforces strict military discipline; John Rolfe begins his experiments in growing West Indies tobacco.

1613—Pocahontas is kidnapped by Samuel Argall.

1614—Pocahontas, converts to Christianity and marries John Rolfe; An eight-year peace between the English and the Powhatan begins; John Rolfe's first tobacco shipment is sent to England.

1616 —Pocahontas sails to England with John
–1617   Rolfe and their son, Thomas; Pocahontas dies; Rolfe, leaving his ill son in England, returns to Jamestown.

1618 —Powhatan dies; The Virginia Company is
–1621   is reorganized; The Great Charter is drawn up; Opechancanough becomes *werowance* of the Powhatan; The first General Assembly meets; A Portuguese ship sells twenty Africans to the colony.

1622 —Opechancanough attacks, killing 347
–1623   colonists; Terrible reprisals are visited on the Powhatan; Colonists die through disease; Only three hundred colonists remain by 1623.

1624 —The Virginia Company dissolves and
–1625   Jamestown becomes a Crown colony; Monthly courts are started which try civil crimes, foreshadowing county courts.

1639 —Charles I approves the calling of general
–1642   assemblies in Virginia.

1644 —Opechancanough's warriors attack again, killing five hundred settlers; The Indian war goes on until 1646, when Opechancanough is captured and then murdered in prison.

1676 —Bacon's Rebellion results in the burning of Jamestown.

1677 —Efforts to rebuild fail; In 1699, the capital of
–1699   Virginia moves to Williamsburg; Jamestown is used by individuals for farming.

★ CHAPTER NOTES ★

Chapter 1. Three Ships Come Sailing In

1. Ivor Noel Hume, *The Virginia Adventure* (New York: Alfred A. Knopf, 1994), p. 130.

2. Warren M. Billings, *Jamestown and the Founding of the Nation* (Gettysburg, Penn.: Thomas Publications, n.d.), p. 15.

3. Ibid., p. 31.

4. Ibid., p. 15.

5. John Smith, "The Founding of Jamestown," *Eyewitness to America: 500 Years of America in the Words of Those Who Saw It Happen,* ed. David Colbert (New York: Pantheon Books, 1997), p. 16.

6. Hume, p. 130.

7. James Axtell, *After Columbus, Essays in the Ethnohistory of Colonial North America* (New York: Oxford University Press, 1988), p. 183.

Chapter 2. New Worlds to Conquer

1. Warren M. Billings, *Jamestown and the Founding of the Nation* (Gettysburg, Penn.: Thomas Publications, n.d.), p. 9.

2. Ivor Noel Hume, *The Virginia Adventure* (New York: Alfred A. Knopf, 1994), p. 6.

3. Billings, p. 10.

4. Hume, p. 7.

5. Ibid., p. 8.

6. Ibid., p. 13.

7. Ibid., p. 23.

8. Ibid., p. 23.

9. John Smith, "The Discovery of Virginia, America," *The Mammoth Book of Eye-Witness History,* ed. Jon E. Lewis (New York: Carroll & Graf Publishers, Inc., 1998), p. 130.

10. Hume, p. 27.

11. James Axtell, *After Columbus, Essays in the Ethnohistory of Colonial North America* (New York: Oxford University Press, 1988), p. 187.

Chapter 3. Crossing the Ocean Blue

1. Clarence L. Ver Steeg and Richard Hofstadter, eds., *Great Issues in American History: From Settlement to Revolution, 1584–1776* (New York: Vintage Books, 1969), vol. 1, p. 24.

2. William Kelso and Beverly Straube, *Jamestown Rediscovery VI* (Jamestown, Va.: The Association for the Preservation of Virginia Antiquities, 2000), p. 7.

3. Ibid., pp. 7–9.

4. Warren M. Billings, *Jamestown and the Founding of the Nation* (Gettysburg, Penn.: Thomas Publications, n.d.), p. 16.

5. Kelso and Straube, p. 3.

6. Ibid., p. 2.

Chapter 4. Captain Smith and Powhatan

1. John Smith, *A History of the Settlement of Virginia* (New York: Maynare, Merrill, & Co., 1890), p. 19.

2. Ibid., p. 5.

3. Ibid., p. 13.

4. Ivor Noel Hume, *The Virginia Adventure* (New York: Alfred A. Knopf, 1994), p. 142.

5. Ibid., p. 142.

6. James Axtell, *After Columbus, Essays in the Ethnohistory of Colonial North America* (New York: Oxford University Press, 1988), p. 184.

7. Smith, p. 45.

8. Axtell, p. 189.

9. Ibid., p. 186.

10. Carl Bridenbaugh, *Jamestown, 1544–1699* (New York: Oxford University Press, 1980), p. 12.

11. Ibid.

Chapter 5. Pocahontas Helps

1. James Axtell, After Columbus, *Essays in the Ethnohistory of Colonial North America* (New York: Oxford University Press, 1988), p. 191.

2. John Smith, *A History of the Settlement of Virginia* (New York: Maynare, Merrill, & Co., 1890), p. 20.

3. Warren M. Billings, *Jamestown and the Founding of the Nation* (Gettysburg, Penn.: Thomas Publications, n.d.), p. 34.

4. Smith, p. 21.

5. Ivor Noel Hume, *The Virginia Adventure* (New York: Alfred A. Knopf, 1994), pp. 172–173.

6. Ibid., p. 174.

7. Ibid., p. 176.

8. Smith, p. 26.

9. John Smith, "Pocahontas Saves John Smith," *Eyewitness to America: 500 Years of America in the Words of Those Who Saw It Happen,* ed. David Colbert (New York: Pantheon Books, 1997), pp. 18–19.

10. Smith, *A History of the Settlement of Virginia*, p. 29.

11. Ibid., p. 179.

12. Hume, p. 179.

13. Ibid., p. 180.

14. Ibid., p. 182.

Chapter 6. Captain Smith in Charge

1. Ivor Noel Hume, *The Virginia Adventure* (New York: Alfred A. Knopf, 1994), p. 187.

2. Ibid.

3. James Axtell, *After Columbus, Essays in the Ethnohistory of Colonial North America* (New York: Oxford University Press, 1988), p. 199.

4. Hume, p. 198.

5. Ibid., pp. 209, 211.

6. Ibid., pp. 195–196.

7. Axtell, p. 203.

8. John Smith, *A History of the Settlement of Virginia* (New York: Maynare, Merrill, & Co., 1890), p. 50.

9. Axtell, p. 200.

10. Ibid.

11. Warren M. Billings, *Jamestown and the Founding of the Nation* (Gettysburg, Penn.: Thomas Publications, n.d.), p. 41.

12. Hume, p. 252.

13. Ibid., p. 235.

14. Virgil Carrington Jones, *Birth of Liberty, The Story of the James River* (New York: Holt, Rinehart and Winston, 1964), p. 40.

15. Hume, p. 251.

Chapter 7. The Starving Time

1. Warren M. Billings, *Jamestown and the Founding of the Nation* (Gettysburg, Penn.: Thomas Publications, n.d.), p. 43.

2. Andrew Cayton, Elisabeth Israels Perry, and Allen M. Winkler, *America: Pathways to the Present* (Needham, Mass.: Prentice Hall, 1995), p. 48.

3. Billings., p. 45.

4. Ivor Noel Hume, *The Virginia Adventure* (New York: Alfred A. Knopf, 1994), p. 243.

5. Ibid., p. 262.

6. Virgil Carrington Jones, *Birth of Liberty, The Story of the James River* (New York: Holt, Rinehart and Winston, 1964), p. 46.

7. Hume, p. 265.

8. Ibid., p. 289.

9. Jones, p. 52.

10. Hume, p. 298.

11. James Axtell, *After Columbus, Essays in the Ethnohistory of Colonial North America* (New York: Oxford University Press, 1988), p. 207.

Chapter 8. John Rolfe and Tobacco

1. Ivor Noel Hume, *The Virginia Adventure* (New York: Alfred A. Knopf, 1994), p. 325.

2. James Axtell, *After Columbus, Essays in the Ethnohistory of Colonial North America* (New York: Oxford University Press, 1988), p. 209.

3. Hume, p. 330.

4. Axtell, p. 210.

5. Hume, p. 348.

6. Thomas Heriot "The Virtues of Tobacco, Virginia," *The Mammoth Book of Eye-Witness History*, ed. Jon E. Lewis (New York: Carroll & Graf Publishers, Inc., 1998), p. 130.

7. Henry Steele Commuger, ed., *Documents of American History*, 6th ed. (New York: Appleton-Century-Crofts, Inc., 1958), Vol. 1, p. 14.

Chapter 9. A New Werowance Makes Plans

1. Virgil Carrington Jones, *Birth of Liberty, The Story of the James River* (New York: Holt, Rinehart and Winston, 1964), p. 69.

2. Warren M. Billings, *Jamestown and the Founding of the Nation* (Gettysburg, Penn.: Thomas Publications, n.d.), p. 51.

3. Ivor Noel Hume, *The Virginia Adventure* (New York: Alfred A. Knopf, 1994), p. 361.

4. James Axtell, *After Columbus, Essays in the Ethnohistory of Colonial North America* (New York: Oxford University Press, 1988), p. 217.

5. Hume, p. 391.

Chapter 10. Jamestown Settles Down

1. James Axtell, *After Columbus, Essays in the Ethnohistory of Colonial North America* (New York: Oxford University Press, 1988), p. 220.

2. Ibid., p. 220.

3. Ivor Noel Hume, *The Virginia Adventure* (New York: Alfred A. Knopf, 1994), p. 394.

Chapter 11. Jamestown Moves On

1. Warren M. Billings, *Jamestown and the Founding of the Nation* (Gettysburg, Penn.: Thomas Publications, n.d.), p. 67.

2. Carl Bridenbaugh, *Jamestown, 1544–1699* (New York: Oxford University Press, 1980), p. 113.

3. Ibid., p. 91.

4. Virgil Carrington Jones, *Birth of Liberty, The Story of the James River* (New York: Holt, Rinehart and Winston, 1964), p. 92.

★ FURTHER READING ★

Books

Britton, Tamara L. *The Virginia Colony.* Minneapolis: ABDO Publishing Co., 2001.

Fritz, Jean. *The Double Life of Pocahontas.* Tarrytown, N.Y.: Marshall Cavendish Co., 1991.

January, Brendan F. *The Jamestown Colony.* Minneapolis: Compass Point Books, 2000.

Mello, Tara Baukus. *John Smith.* Broomall, Pa.: Chelsea House Publishers, 1999.

Sakurai, Gail. *The Jamestown Colony.* Danbury, Conn.: Children's Press, 1997.

Sullivan, George E. *Pocahontas.* New York: Scholastic, Inc., 2001.

Internet Addresses

Association for the Preservation of Virginia Antiquities. "Jamestown Rediscovery." April 16, 2001. <http://www.apva.org/jr.html>.

Kehrberg, Kirk D. "Jamestown Historic Briefs." *National Park Service: Colonial National Historic Park.* July 11, 2001. <http://www.nps.gov/colo/Jthanout/JTBriefs.html>.

Shifflett, Crandall. "Virtual Jamestown." *The Institute for Advanced Technology in the Humanities.* 2000. <http://www.iath.virginia.edu/vcdh/jamestown/page2.html>.

★ INDEX ★

A

Amadas, Philip, 20, 21, 22
Appomattox Indians, 76
Archer, Gabriel, 49, 64, 66
Argall, Samuel, 64, 75, 76, 82, 83, 87, 88
Aviles, Pedro Menendez de, 36, 37
Axtell, James, 35, 36, 80

B

Bacon, Nathaniel, Jr., 111, 112
Barlowe, Arthur, 20, 21, 22
Berkeley, William, 100, 101, 104, 105, 106, 108, 109, 111, 112
Billings, Warren M., 70
Borough, Stephen, 17
Bridenbaugh, Carl, 36

C

Cabot, John, 15, 17
Cabot, Sebastian, 15, 17
Cartier, Jacques, 15
Cassen, George, 44
Chancellor, Richard, 17
Charles I, king of England, 97, 98, 101, 104, 105, 106, 107, 108
Charles II, king of England, 106, 108, 109, 112
Chickahominy Indians, 34, 84
Chickahominy River, 43, 81
Columbus, Christopher, 14
Cromwell, Oliver, 105

D

Dale, Thomas, 69, 78, 79, 80, 84, 85, 86, 87, 88
Dee, John, 17
De La Warr, Lord, 65, 66, 69, 73, 74, 76–78, 82, 89
Deliverance, 71
Discovery, 7, 26, 42, 49, 72, 114, 116
Divers Voyages Touching the Discovery of America, 20
Drake, Francis, 17

E

Elizabeth I, queen of England, 19, 20, 24
Emry, Thomas, 44, 49

F

Frobisher, Martin, 18

G

Gabriel, 18
Gates, Thomas, 24, 64, 65, 69, 71, 73, 75, 77, 78, 80, 82, 85
General Assembly, 89, 107, 109, 111, 113
Generall Historie of Virginia, 59
Gilbert, Humphrey, 18, 19
Godspeed, 7, 26, 40, 41, 114, 116
Golden Hind, 19
Gosnold, Bartholomew, 12, 26, 30
Grenville, Richard, 21

H

Hakluyt, Richard, 19–20, 21
Harvey, John, 100
Hawkins, John, 17
Henrico, 80, 84, 86, 111
Henry, Prince of Wales, 80
History of the Settlement of Virginia, A, 31
Hog Island, 62
Hume, Ivor, 104

I

Iapazaws, 83
Itopatin, 92

J

Jack of the Feather, 80, 94, 95
James I, king of England, 7, 9, 12, 24, 33, 41, 60, 61, 65, 85, 96, 97
James River, 5, 7, 8, 13, 28, 29, 33, 34, 54, 62, 63, 66, 78, 81, 87, 98, 101, 105, 108, 112, 114, 118
John and Francis, 50
Jones, Virgil, 113

K

Kecoughtan Indians, 28, 34
Kelso, William, 28
Kendall, George, 12, 41

L

Lawes Divine, Morall and Martiall, 79, 89

M
Martin, John, 12, 59, 66
More, Thomas, 17

N
Newport, Christopher, 12, 13, 27, 29, 30, 32, 33, 34, 39, 41, 50, 51, 53, 54, 57, 58, 60, 61, 62, 63, 69, 75, 77
New World, 7, 9, 14, 15, 16, 17, 24, 77, 100, 118
Nicholson, Francis, 113
Northwest Passage, 9, 15, 18, 24, 30, 56

O
Occaneechi Indians, 103, 111
Opechancanough, 22, 36, 37, 38, 45, 47, 59, 68, 92, 93, 94, 95, 97, 103, 104

P
Pamunkey Indians, 45
Parahunt, 33
Paspahegh Indians, 8, 13, 29, 39, 40, 42, 53
Patawomeke Indians, 82, 83
Patience, 71
Percy, George, 29, 42, 59, 76, 82
Philip II, king of Spain, 37
Phoenix, 50, 55, 56
Plymouth Colony, 99
Pocahontas, 46, 47, 49, 55, 82, 83, 86
Popham, John, 24
Powhatan, 33, 34, 35, 35, 36, 42, 46, 47, 49, 54, 55, 58, 60, 61, 68, 70, 76, 79, 81, 82–83, 84, 92, 94
Powhatan Indians, 8, 13, 36, 37, 59, 76

R
Raleigh, Walter, 19, 20, 21
Rastell, John, 17
Ratcliffe, John, 12, 41, 49, 56, 62, 64, 66, 70
Roanoke Island, 21, 22, 53, 54
Robinson, John, 44, 49
Rolfe, John, 81, 83, 84, 86, 87, 93, 95
Rolfe, Thomas, 86, 87
Rut, John, 17

S
Sandys, Edwin, 89, 93, 96
Scrivener, Matthew, 56
Sea Venture, 69, 71, 72

Smith, John, 12–13, 31, 32, 35, 38, 39, 41, 42, 43–47, 49, 50, 51, 54, 55, 56, 57, 58, 59, 60, 61, 62–63, 64, 65, 66, 68, 69–70, 73, 82, 86, 100
Smythe, Thomas, 24, 89
Somers, George, 65, 69, 71, 75, 76
Starving Time, the, 70, 73, 77
Strachey, William, 71, 72, 79
Susan Constant, 7, 26, 30, 39, 41, 116
Susquehannock Indians, 110, 111

T
Thorpe, George, 92, 95
tobacco, 81, 84, 85, 87, 88, 89, 90, 91, 98, 99, 108, 109
Treasurer, 82

U
Utopia, 17

V
Vaughan, Robert, 59
Velasco, Don Luis de, 37
Verrazano, Giovanni da, 17
Vespucci, Amerigo, 16
Virginia, 72
Virginia Company, 10, 24, 26, 41, 60, 62, 64, 65, 77, 79, 82, 89, 96, 101

W
Wahunsonacock. *See* Powhatan.
Waldseemüller, Martin, 17
werowance, 8, 33, 34, 55, 60, 92
West, Thomas, 65
William III, king of England, 113
Williamsburg, 113, 118
Willoughby, Hugh, 17
Wingfield, Edward Maria, 12, 13, 24, 39, 41
Wyatt, Francis, 93, 95, 96

Y
Yeardley, George, 87, 89, 93, 94
York River, 45, 46, 54